EYES WIDE OPEN

THE POWER OF CLEAR SPIRITUAL VISION

TERRY LEWIS

EQUIP PRESS
COLORADO SPRINGS, COLORADO

Eyes Wide Open: The Powerful of Clear Spiritual Vision
Copyright © 2018 by Terry Lewis
All rights reserved. No part of this publication may be reproduced, distributed, or transmitted in any form or by any means, without prior written permission.

Published by Equip Press, Colorado Springs, CO

Scripture quotations marked (ESV) are taken from *The ESV® Bible (The Holy Bible, English Standard Version®)* copyright © 2001 by Crossway, a publishing minis-try of Good News Publishers. ESV® Text Edition: 2011. The ESV® text has been reproduced in cooperation with and by permission of Good News Publishers. Unauthorized reproduction of this publication is prohibited. Used by permission. All rights reserved.

Scripture quotations marked (KJV) are taken from the *King James Bible*. Accessed on Bible Gateway at www.BibleGateway.com.

Scripture quotations marked (NASB) are taken from the *New American Standard Bible®* (NASB), copyright © 1960, 1962, 1963, 1968, 1971, 1972, 1973, 1975, 1977, 1995 by The Lockman Foundation, www.Lockman.org. Used by permission.

Scripture quotations marked (NIV) are taken from the *Holy Bible, New International Version*. Copyright © 1973, 1978, 1984, 2011 by Biblica, Inc.® Used by permission. All rights reserved worldwide.

Scripture quotations marked (NKJV) are taken from the *New King James Version®*. Copyright © 1982 by Thomas Nelson, Inc. Used by permission. All rights reserved.

Scripture quotations marked (NLT) are taken from the *Holy Bible, New Living Translation*, copyright © 1996, 2004, 2015 by Tyndale House Foundation. Used by permission of Tyndale House Publishers, Inc., Carol Stream, Illinois 60188. All rights reserved.

Scripture quotations marked (NRSV) are taken from the *New Revised Standard Version Bible*, copyright © 1989 the Division of Christian Education of the National Council of the Churches of Christ in the United States of America. Used by permission. All rights reserved.

First Edition 2018
Eyes Wide Open: The Powerful of Clear Spiritual Vision / Terry Lewis
Paperback ISBN: 978-1-946453-19-8
eBook ISBN: 978-1-946453-20-4

To Tresa, the love of my life:
Thank you for believing in me and encouraging me in every step of life and ministry. You are a beautiful and amazing wife, mother, "Mamay," friend, and an anointed Woman of God. I would not be who I am today without you. You are my always and forever.

To Corey, Matt, and Alaka:
I am proud to call you my kids and my best friends. Thank you for sharing our lives and our time with others. The greatest gift of my life is being your Dad.

To Reagan:
You are Poppa's sidekick! I love you to the moon and back.

To our parents,
Bernall & Martha Lewis and Jerry & Betty Parks:
I have known nothing my entire life but praying parents who love the Lord and love their children. We will always know what it means to be a true Christian by watching your lives.

To my family:
Glinda, Don, David, Dean, Rodney, and all my favorite nieces and nephews — I love you.

CONTENTS

Acknowledgments	7
Prologue	9
Focus	13
Be Happy in Your Faith	23
Open Line of Communication	29
Give Thanks in Everything	59
Heartburn	77
The Prophetic Word	93
Embrace the Good Stuff	101
The Grace-Covered Life	117
A Changed Mind	127
Epilogue	130

ACKNOWLEDGMENTS

With all of my being, I am thankful to Jesus Christ, the Lord of my life, for His grace continually shown to me.

The opportunity to pastor the great FaithPointe family is a daily gift to my life. I cannot express with words the gratitude in my heart for this beautiful family of dear friends that I get to worship with each week. Your belief and support of our vision, your passion for the Word, and the atmosphere of love and worship in our House make us beautifully unique. The FaithPointe staff, my assistants, the leadership team and volunteers are the greatest in the world — you make me look really good!

I am grateful to every pastor who has graciously received me in their pulpit in the past 30 years. It is an honor that I forever respect. You have encouraged Tresa and me far more than we have ever helped you. I honor your gifts as men and women of God.

I give honor to Bishop James and Mimi Rayburn for your faithful and humble leadership. You are great examples of integrity to all of us in the Pentecostal Church of God, and especially the Kentucky District.

To Pastor Tommy & Hallie Schooler and Rev. Bobby & Hazel Centers — thank you for believing in me as a young preacher. I am forever grateful for the opportunities you extended to me when I had no clue what I was doing.

To the great pastors who serve on our Pastor's Board of Advisors, whose friendship and insight we sincerely value:

Pastor Ed & Linda Jarrell, Full Gospel Tabernacle, Lima, Ohio

Pastor Winston & Jeri McClurg, House of Prayer, Morehead, Kentucky

Pastor Asa & Debbie Dockery, World Harvest Church North, Blairsville, Georgia

Pastor Shaun & Te-Kisha Ferguson, Faith Temple Christian Center, Rockledge, Florida

To Ron Gray — my marketing specialist and friend for life.

To Bill Smith — your friendship and generosity helped bring the FaithPointe dream to reality.

To Lena, Rebecca, and Steven — thank you for giving unselfishly of your time with this book project. Your assistance and suggestions are greatly appreciated.

To Rick Barnes — Thank you for adopting us and for always being there, wherever and whenever.

PROLOGUE

The rattling of chains and the groans of the injured and abused have become my daily wake-up call. I know too well the feeling of pain mingled with the uncertainty that permeates the darkness of the regions below my cell.

A sliver of sunlight is peeking through the window near my head. It has been a long time since I have breathed the fresh air of the outdoors. A rumble in my stomach reminds me that it also has been a long time since our last meal. Not that a few pieces of moldy bread would be called a meal, but I would be grateful for anything about now.

It is early and I treasure this time. I sense the presence of the Lord even as I begin to whisper one of my favorite of David's songs:

"I will praise thee with my whole heart: before the gods will I sing praise unto thee. I will worship toward Thy holy temple, and praise Thy name for Thy lovingkindness and for Thy truth: for Thou hast magnified Thy word above all Thy name.

In the day when I cried Thou answeredst me, and strengthenedst me with strength in my soul. All the kings of the earth shall praise Thee, O LORD, when they hear the words of Thy mouth. Yea, they shall sing in the ways of the LORD: for great is the glory of the LORD.

Though the LORD be high, yet hath He respect unto the lowly: but the proud He knoweth afar off. Though I walk in the midst of trouble, Thou wilt revive me: Thou shalt stretch forth Thine hand against the wrath of mine enemies, and Thy right hand shall save me.

*The L*ORD *will perfect that which concerneth me: Thy mercy, O L*ORD*, endureth for ever: forsake not the works of thine own hands."* [1]

Oh, how wonderful is His presence in this place! Though my eyesight has grown dim and my hands are shaky, I still vividly remember when my precious Savior began to speak to my hard heart. Though my mind was filled with a zealous commitment to stop those who boldly proclaimed the gospel of a risen Christ, my heart would beat loudly when I heard their declarations of salvation in the marketplace. My fellow Pharisees knew nothing of my inner turmoil, of course. And to think I would even consider taking one moment's heed to their teachings! Even as I personally demanded the authority to stop this heresy, the turmoil in my heart confirmed what I was ashamed to admit. Jesus Christ was the Messiah. I saw Him in my dreams. I heard His words when I awoke. Though my face was stoic, I grieved inwardly as the mob stoned precious Stephen for his testimony. And the moment he looked toward heaven, and said, "I see Jesus standing at the right hand of God," I knew. I knew.

Our encounter on the Damascus Road. His healing touch through the obedience of Ananias. Planting churches and home meetings. The power of the Christ manifested through signs, wonders, and miracles. The many faces of joyous believers in our precious Lord scroll through my mind encouraging my soul daily. Silvanus, Barnabas, Titus, and Philemon. Lucius, Jason, Sosispater, Tertius, Gaius, Erastus, and Quartus. Godly women who have been great leaders in every way — Priscilla, Mary, Persis, Phoebe, Chloe — along with Lois and Eunice and many others, without whom this gospel could not have touched our world. Perhaps I should not have favorites, but my soul has been often encouraged by my dear sons in the faith, Timothy and Demas.

Let me get about, now. Today may be the day that the young jailer's assistant may bow on his knees and come to the same knowledge of salvation by grace through faith in Jesus the Christ, just as me! He has asked many questions of late. I pray that he will surrender to the Lord while his heart is still tender to the insistent tug of the Spirit of God. Yes, today is the day! Perhaps Timothy or Demas will visit me today. Together we can shine the glorious light of the gospel to this young man. I must not allow this opportunity to pass me by. Who knows how many more days I will be in this place? Who knows how many more days I will have on this earth? Lord, give me Your words of eternal life to speak to this young man, and to all who will hear me. Amen.

"Paul? Brother Paul?" I hear the hushed words of dear Timothy near the window. "Yes, young Timothy, my son." As I press my face into the bars of the window, the sight of this young man of faith brings joy to my morning. Even in my bonds, he remains my faithful companion. He says that our time together is an encouragement to him. In actuality, it is quite the opposite. Lois and Eunice, his mother and grandmother, have raised a fine young man who will be a great evangelist for the Lord Jesus Christ.

As I slip my hands through the bars to join him in a psalm and prayer, I see that his face looks sorrowful. "Timothy, why are you troubled? You look as if you have been weeping. Is it your grandmother? Your mother?"

"Paul, I have something to tell you...."

CHAPTER 1

FOCUS

It was in the second grade that my parents began to notice that I was doing something they called "squinting." A visit to the optometrist confirmed what they already knew — I needed glasses. From the age of seven until the present, I make an annual visit to the "eye doctor," watching the screen as the rows of letters come and go out of focus as he adjusts the equipment. "Which one is clearer, one or two?" My doctor says I am legally blind without glasses or contacts. Without them, everything is blurry. Thankfully, my vision can be corrected to 20./20. The contact lenses I put in each eye every morning bring everything into focus. I value the gift of sight — the ability to clearly see the physical reality of all things around me.

From a spiritual viewpoint, vision takes on a much different perspective. I am not referring to visions (the experience of seeing something supernatural), but of spiritual vision — *the focus of our heart.* Where your focus goes is where your power goes. The enemy of our soul (Satan, Lucifer, the devil, whatever you want to call him) is a defeated foe. When Jesus cried, "It is finished," it forever determined that every one of us can live absolutely victorious over that enemy. We do know that our enemy has influence in the world, and that is why that we must be aware and vigilant so that his influence does not spill over into our lives. His goal is *to "steal, and to kill, and to destroy"* (Matthew 10:10). He wants to destroy your destiny, he wants to destroy your purpose, and he wants you to be separated from the Divine leadership of the Holy Spirit. He would be satisfied with you wandering aimlessly, making mistakes and mishaps. He wants to steal your joy, your faith, your family, your finances, and everything else that is precious to you.

While we are busily living our lives, our enemy is busy plotting our destruction. *"Be sober, be vigilant; because your adversary the devil, as a roaring lion, walks about, seeking whom he may devour"* (1 Peter 5:8). He will set you up today to destroy you months from now. This tells me that if he has plans for my destruction, I must have plans for my protection. We are not to give him any space. As the old adage says, "If you give him an inch, he will take a mile." We cannot let down our guard, we cannot spiritually relax, and we will not allow the enemy to win in our lives.

If you know that your enemy is shooting at you, then you should stop loading his gun. What does that mean? The way you load his gun is with your mouth. Satan is not omnipotent or omniscient — he is not everywhere and he does not know everything — but he does know what he hears, and he listens to what you say. Whatever negative thing you reveal to him, he will magnify in your life. When you constantly talk about what makes you angry, or the people you do not like, or how bad you feel, or how worried you are, or how upset you are, you have just exposed those areas as weaknesses. "I just feel so bad that I don't think I can hardly make it," is a sure way to feel even worse. "She gets on my nerves; I just can't stand her," is a sure way to have her in your face every day.

I am victorious when I can keep my mouth shut against everything negative, not speaking doubt into my life. My victory is to speak faith into my life, and the things that I speak faith to are the things that I need strength in. The Bible says, *"'Let the weak say that I am strong'"* (Joel 3:10). Whatever area you are struggling in is where you should speak the Word of God in your life the most. You do not have to be in church to testify, and you do not have to be in church to speak the Word. You can speak the Word in your home, your car, when you are mowing the yard, and when you are pushing a cart through a grocery store! It does not matter where you are!

When you speak the Word of faith to a thing, it comes into agreement with His Word, in Jesus name.

When you speak the Word of God, something has to change. The Bible says that the Word does not return void (Isaiah 55:11). "Well, I've been praying about something and it did not happen." Have you been praying the Word, or have you just been worrying about it? Too often we have things on our minds, and we talk to our friends about it, and we talk to our church buddies about it, and we talk to Momma about it, but we never actually talk to God about it ... yet we call that prayer! That is not prayer — that is worry. Or even worse, that is attention-seeking. The way I talk to God about it is through prayer and by speaking the Word! If I am sick, I speak healing to my body. How do we do that? "Father, I thank You that by the stripes of Jesus Christ I am healed! I praise You that no weapon formed against me shall prosper! I praise You that Jesus took stripes for my healing at Calvary, and I do not have to be sick, but I am healed. I praise You that I am not going to be destroyed by sickness, but I am going to walk in health and healing!"

If you have a financial problem, then you begin to speak faith to your finances. How do we do that? "Father, I thank You that I am blessed as a spiritual seed of Abraham. My finances are blessed, my wallet is blessed, my checkbook is blessed, my bank account is blessed. I praise You that I am the lender and not the borrower! Since I am a faithful tither, I thank You that my enemy cannot destroy what God has given me. He will not destroy my seed nor destroy my harvest. I praise You that I am blessed going in and I am blessed going out. I am blessed in the country and I am blessed in the city. Everything that I put my hand to is blessed." When you start speaking that Word into your life, I assure you that your finances will turn around! The Word shows us time and again that if you are a giver, you are blessed!

If you are having problems with your children, don't tell them how bad they are, but instead, tell them how blessed they are! Negativity and name-calling do nothing positive for them or their future. We do not curse our children; we bless them. How do I do that? "You are blessed, you are anointed, you are a child of God! You are not a failure, you are not a mistake, and you are not going to be led astray by the enemy. You are the blessed of God, the anointed of the Lord, you have been called of God, you are the apple of His eye! You are His beloved and His banner over you is love. Angels have been given charge over you. You are called to sit in heavenly places in Christ Jesus!" When you speak that Word over their lives, I promise you that something great is going to happen in your kids!

Furthermore, making declarations of His Word not only brings the blessing in our lives, it also brings revelation. The Bible says we should regularly practice a spiritual self-examination (1 Corinthians 11:28). The number one person that I have to keep an eye on is me. I need to focus on me — not my neighbor, not my church friends — on me! I am a full-time job for me. I have enough work taking care of myself without trying to fix others. "Well, Pastor, are you suggesting there is something wrong with me?" Yep — there is something wrong with all of us! Only two men in the Bible, Enoch and Elijah, walked so closely to God that they were caught away in their own personal rapture. Since you and I are still here, there must be some things for us to work on. The last thing we need is a church full of people busily trying to show each other how impressive we are. Sorry, but we have no time for "look how anointed I am." We all are a process. We all need work. The great Apostle Paul said, *"For I know that in me (that is, in my flesh) nothing good dwells …."* (Romans 7:18). I have nothing to bring to the table to impress God. The only thing that I can bring to God is this: I have been covered by the Blood of Jesus, I am a child of God, royal blood flows through my veins, and it has nothing to do with me, but it has everything to do with Him. All I can bring is faith.

My responsibility is to examine myself and make sure that every single part of me is covered by His Blood, His mercy, and His grace. As for the places in my life that need work, I want to examine myself and say, "God, You can work on me. Work on my mouth, my temper, my anger, my lust, my stinginess, and my selfishness. Bring revelation, O God, to anything that is not right with You. Put the spotlight of your

Word on any area of vulnerability, weakness, or failure in my heart. I give You permission because I want to walk in right-standing with You!" And to someone who may say, "Well, Pastor, I just do not know if I am right with God or not," my answer is, "Sure you do!" There are always two who know about your spiritual condition — you and God. We used to sing a song years ago in the Holiness churches, "You can hide it from the preacher, but you sure can't hide it from God; can't nobody hide!"[2] That may sound a little unusual if you did not have that kind of church background, but it is actually the truth — you cannot hide from God. That is not a comment of fear because I am not afraid of God. But, I am afraid of me! Many spend a lifetime being afraid of God, and He is not the one to fear. God is the only One who loves me completely. If I am going to be afraid of something, I ought to be afraid of my own foolishness. God said, *"My people are destroyed for lack of knowledge"* (Hosea 4:6). Churches have never been destroyed because of demons and devils. They cannot cross the Blood line! We can never be destroyed by the sheer will of the devil, but we can be destroyed by ignorance, foolishness, and stubbornness. We can be destroyed or led astray by our vulnerabilities. *"But each one is tempted when he is drawn away by his own desires and enticed"* (James 1:14).

The enemy of our soul is looking for that one spot to destroy us, and our weak spot will be his area of exploitation. He is the master of making a mountain out of a molehill. The smallest of weaknesses can be made to look like the biggest of mountains, convincing us that we cannot have victory, and that we will never get over this, and we cannot live right, and this will never work out right, and we might as well give up, and might as well quit trying to live for God ... it is all a lie! There is not anything in our lives in which we cannot be victorious. He went to the cross to cover every problem that we will ever face. Every situation has already been taken care of at Christ's cross. The only way that it will destroy us is if we allow the enemy to exploit that weakness instead of allowing the Holy Ghost to put His power in that spot and give us victory in Jesus name.

We should ask God to give us the spirit of discernment. Not primarily discernment about others — the person I want to discern is me. Some "super spiritual" people professing that gift may not really have the spirit of discernment; they have the spirit of nosiness. They have the spirit of "mind your business" instead of the spirit of self-examination. If I am going to have discernment about someone, I want to know what is going on with me. Where is my short-coming? Where is my problem? Where is my weakness? Why do I keep failing in this area? Why does this keep bothering me? Why can I not get victory over this? Why do I keep falling into that kind of mess? The gift of discernment is a powerful and valuable gift used by the Holy Ghost to cover and protect the church. But for every one of us concerned about our own personal spiritual growth, do not get discernment about your brother or sister; get discernment about you and where you are with God.

LIVING IN HIS PRESENCE

"He who dwells in the secret place of the Most High shall abide under the shadow of the Almighty" (Psalm 91:1). This is a powerful Scripture that demonstrates the power of God's spiritual protection. Perhaps this verse was on the mind of Christ when He cried out, *"O Jerusalem, Jerusalem, the one who kills the prophets and stones those who are sent to her! How often I wanted to gather your children together, as a hen gathers her chicks under her wings, but you were not willing"* (Matthew 23:37). The religious folks of His day were too busy saying, "You can't be the Christ, because you do not look like us, and you do not fit our description of a prophet, and you were not born in the right place to the right people." His contemporaries were busily looking at Jesus from Nazareth, instead of allowing Jesus the Word to focus on them. They crucified The Man on the cross, Who was the only Man they truly needed while He was with them. But, some believed. And, they only believed when they quit looking at Jesus and began listening to Jesus. To everyone that heard, believed, and received His Word, He changed their lives. I submit to you that what He did, He is still doing

now. When our natural eyes are off of people and things and our spiritual eyes are on Him, our lives will be changed.

"I will say of the Lord, 'He is my refuge and my fortress; My God, in Him will I trust'" (Psalm 91:2). When we live in the presence of God, we will abide (permanent residence). In His presence is the secure place of trust. What does it mean to live in His presence? Is that the person who sings the loudest, dances the most, testifies the best, and prays the longest in our church services? No. Living in His presence means that Jesus Christ is the Lord of your life. When we live in His presence, Christ is in charge. Life is not about me, it is about Him.

Unfortunately, some church folk say (by actions, not usually by words), "Look how anointed I am. Look how great I am." Those self-absorbed, self-righteous types have just made their flesh the lord of their lives. When we say, "Look at me," that says it is our flesh in charge. This often occurs when we start following the compliments and accolades of men. As long as it is all "me, me, me," then that is who my lord is — me. When Christ is the Lord of my life and my life is not about me, then everything is about Him. Our testimony is, "look what the Lord has done!"

When Jesus was asked about John the Baptist, He made this declaration: *"For I say to you, among those born of women there is not a greater prophet than John the Baptist; but he who is least in the kingdom of God is greater than he"* (Luke 7:28). Wow! That is a great compliment, isn't it? Jesus says that John was the greatest man who ever lived. If you are John the Baptist, it might be challenging to stay humble. But, here is what John the Baptist said: *"'He must increase, but I must decrease'"* (John 3:30). Why did John say this? *"And they came to John and said to him, 'Rabbi, He who was with you beyond the Jordan, to Whom you have testified — behold, He is baptizing, and all are coming to Him'"* (John 3:26).

John's disciples and followers are either confused or upset because Jesus is now getting all the attention. If you are a pastor and your members come running to you, saying, "Reverend Superpreacher has a church on the other side of town and now everyone is going over there," your flesh wants to have one of those *who-does-he-think-he-is* moments. "I have been in this town longer than he has. We have been faithful, we have sacrificed, and we have paid our dues, bless God!" When they came to John the Baptist, they said, "Hey, John … you know that guy that you baptized, with the dove and the lightning and the voice from heaven and all that? He is over there having church now and they are baptizing and teaching and packing 'em in! We're losing our crowds. Offerings are down. We have competition!" But, *"John answered and said, 'A man can receive nothing unless it has been given to him from heaven. You yourselves bear me witness that I said, "I am not the Christ, but, I have been sent before Him." He who has the bride is the groom; but the friend of the groom, who stands and hears him, rejoices greatly because of the groom's voice. Therefore this joy of mine is fulfilled. He must increase, but I must decrease'"* (John 3:27-30).

What would John say to today's church? "If there is a church where people are receiving salvation, healing, and deliverance, then it does not matter if it is my church, his church, her church; we celebrate! We are all on the same team, playing for the same Coach, building the same Kingdom. There are enough people who need salvation, without me worrying about who is joining what church. It is not about my name, my agenda, or me; it is about God being God and changing lives. It is not about me!" It is our great honor to be the planters and pastors of FaithPointe, but FaithPointe is not about Terry and Tresa Lewis. When people leave to attend a different church, as long as it is not because of offense or negligence on our part, our only response should be to praise God. When people walk away from us, then they are no longer assigned to us. They are moving to a new level in their Christ-walk. This is not a competition!

The more we decrease the more He increases. When Jesus is made the Lord of our lives, we put Him in complete control. When all we do is all about Him, the enemy loses. Satan cannot destroy us, separate us, bring division, or bring schisms without our permission. We all abide in unity in His secret place. The Holy Spirit keeps us protected under the shadow of the Almighty and that is where the safety is — in the presence of God. He becomes the Lord of how we act, the way we think, the things we do, and everything we are about. He is The Lord, and when He is given complete control and full access, blessings are revealed in our lives that had not even been dreamed about. When we pray in secret, He will reward us openly. When we seek Him in humility, He will raise us up to high places. We no longer care about someone knowing our name or what we can do. When Jesus Christ is the Lord of our lives, He will open doors that no one can shut, and shut doors that no one can open. His anointing will be magnified through our lives.

Our decisions regarding our life in Christ are of eternal impact. Quite literally, our decisions indicate whether or not we want to go to heaven. If you are going to live for God, the time is NOW. Our world continues in chaos as the glorious church is propelled ever closer to the second coming of Christ. That is not a contradictory statement: before the church leaves, the world is going to get worse and the church is going to get better. Christ is not returning for a church that is limping through the last days. Jesus said, "I am coming back for a glorious church" (Ephesians 3:27). So as the world falls apart, the church is seeing the glory of the Lord in greater measure than we have known for decades. I do believe that we are in a time of revival. I do believe that we are going to see more people saved, healed, delivered, and filled than we ever have. I do believe that the best days of the church are ahead of us. But, I also believe this — the devil knows all of that, too. If he is working against us, we must have a sharper focus, renewed determination, and fervent zeal — a united army that is full of the Holy Ghost and power. We are keenly aware of our time, as *"the spirit of Antichrist, which you have heard was coming ... is now already in the world"* (1 John 4:3). Is that disturbing? Perhaps, but not disconcerting — *"you are from God, little children and have overcome them, because He who is in you is greater than he who is in the world"* (1 John 4:4). God has a plan, we have the authority!

Our enemy has an influence in the world, and we must be aware and vigilant so that his influence will not spill over into our lives. Jesus said, *"The thief does not come except to steal, and to kill, and to destroy. I have come that they may have life, and that they may have it more abundantly"* (John 10:10). We are determined to walk in the abundant life and not have anything stolen. The enemy wants to destroy our destiny, our purpose, and ultimately, to separate us from the Divine leadership of the Holy Spirit. If you are a born-again Believer, the devil cannot have your soul, nor does he have any access to your salvation. What he can do is influence our focus, and watch us wander aimlessly through life, not fulfilling the destiny and purpose that God ordained for our lives.

In the following chapters, allow me to expound on seven short but powerful verses from 1 Thessalonians 5:16-22, that I believe are critical keys to the power of clear spiritual vision.

[16] Rejoice always, [17] pray without ceasing, [18] in everything give thanks; for this is the will of God in Christ Jesus for you.
[19] Do not quench the Spirit. [20] Do not despise prophecies. [21] Test all things; hold fast what is good. [22] Abstain from every form of evil.

CHAPTER 2

BE HAPPY IN YOUR FAITH

"Rejoice evermore." The Amplified Version of the Bible says: *"Be happy in your faith."* You have permission to be happy. In the words of *Duck Dynasty* star, Phil Robertson, be "Happy, happy, happy!" You have both the permission and exhortation to be happy. You have been covered by the blood of Jesus, and you cannot get a life any better than that! In Luke 10, the Bible says that Jesus sent out 70 disciples to proclaim the gospel of the Kingdom before His most extensive ministry campaign. When they returned from their evangelistic journeys, they eagerly shared with Jesus of their great success. *"Lord, even the demons are subject to us in Your name"* (Luke 10:17). While I am sure Jesus shared in their excitement, He wanted them to remain focused on the primary mission of His life. Jesus said, *"… Do not rejoice in this, that the spirits are subject to you, but rather rejoice because your names are written in Heaven"* (Luke 10:20). Rejoice! You cannot get any more blessed than being a saved child of God! If you are a born-again believer, you cannot help but be "happy, happy, happy!" Do not attach your identity to confusion, drama, and pity parties when your name is written down in the Lamb's Book of Life. Be happy knowing that through Christ your sins have not only been forgiven, *"He has removed our sins as far from us as the east is from the west"* (Psalm 103:12, NLT). Be Happy! There is no way that you should have the same countenance as those unsaved people you hang out with, work with, and that you are related to. There is no way that you ought to look like they look, who do not know the hope and joy and promise you have by grace through faith in Christ. I know Who ordains my life plan, and I now know Who holds my tomorrow. I have a reason to

smile, and shout and be happy even if nobody else has one. You have the right to say "Praise the Lord," no matter what.

What about the bad days? That's a fair question because we all have them. In one day, the great patriarch Job lost everything he had. In one day, Job and his wife experienced unfathomable loss. In one day, all of their oxen and mules were stolen and their farmhands murdered. The same day, a wildfire came through their property and killed all of their sheep and the shepherds who were tending them. The same day, all of their camels were stolen by a band of enemy soldiers, and the workers who tended them were killed. Later the same day, their seven sons and three daughters were having dinner at the oldest brother's home when a tornado came through and killed all ten of them. This all happened on the same day. How do you lose all your children and everything you own in one day and without warning? The profound grief of this couple is quite understandable, when *"Job arose, tore his robe, and shaved his head...."* What is not so understandable is what he does next: *"... and he fell to the ground and worshiped"* (Job 1:20). After this great loss, Job becomes very ill with painful boils that covered his entire body. Now, Mrs. Job feels as if she has gone above and beyond in the faith and trust department. *"Then his wife said to him, 'Do you still hold fast to your integrity? Curse God and die!'"* Yet, throughout their great calamity, Job continues to proclaim, *"'Blessed be the name of the Lord.' Job did not sin nor charge God with wrong"* (Job 1:21-22).

When we say "God is good," that does not mean God is good only when we have money in our pocket. That does not mean God is good only when we feel good. That does not mean God is good only when we have the keys to a new car. God is good all the time. And all the time, God is good! In any given day of our lives, we know that God has blessed us too much, made a way too often, has covered us too great, has moved mountains for us too powerfully, has opened doors of favor for us too extensively, and has shut the doors of a painful history for us too emphatically. That is way "too much" for us to pout, frown, and worry! I think some folks are watching reruns of "Hee Haw", with its woeful classic song as their personal anthem: *"Gloom, despair, and agony on me! Deep dark depression, excessive misery! If it weren't for bad luck I'd have no luck at all! Gloom, despair, and agony on me!"*[3] Permit me to be bold — get that junk out of your life! Let me give you a much better song, written by Israel Houghton, directly from Philippians 4:4: *"Rejoice in the Lord always, And again I say, and again I say, Rejoice!"*[4] Emphatically declare, "I am a child of the King, royal blood flows through my veins, and I know I am born again!"

I am not a morning person. I do not understand morning people. They are up two hours before work, in the gym, walking the dog, meeting friends for coffee … you know the type … they bounce into work with a big smile and an exaggerated "Good Morning!" that is a little too loud and way too enthusiastic. I usually want to walk the other way. Imagine how the devil feels when it seems he has thrown everything but the kitchen sink at you this week, and you still show up in the house of God, tears rolling off your face, hands raised in worship, and you boldly and honestly say, "Thank God." If there is such a thing as "putting the devil on the run," that will do it. And, more importantly, what does that do for you? It shifts your focus from the problems to The Solution. (Cue Bobby McFerrin: *"Don't Worry, Be Happy!"*) Having a bad day, a bad week, or maybe you think you have had a bad year? Perhaps everything in your life is not going the way you think it is supposed to right now? The temporary things on the outside have absolutely nothing to do with the miracle God has performed on the inside.

Consider our Lord the night before He was to be tried, convicted, and sentenced to die. He looked at His bewildered disciples and said, *"These things I have spoken to you, that my joy may remain in you, and that your joy may be full"* (John 15:11). Who could possibly be thinking about joy when you are hours away from the cross? The answer to that is, from one whose joy is inwardly established and outwardly impacted. Outward circumstances can trouble our minds but never touch our spirit. Herein lies the great treasure of a steadfast relationship with God. I have considered many times Paul's encouraging words, as he discussed the challenges of life and the sustaining power of his faith: *"We are hard-pressed on every side, yet not crushed; we are perplexed, but not in despair; persecuted, but not forsaken; struck down, but not destroyed"* (2 Corinthians 4:8-9).

Let's go back to Job for a minute — picture him sitting in a Christian counselor's office, in deep crisis and profound grief. Remember that he has lost all of his possessions and all of his children were killed in a freak windstorm in the same day. On the other side of the table is the Christian counselor, who listens intently to all of Job's losses in that horrific day, and then plainly says, "Well, you should stop crying now. Don't you know that the Bible says, "Rejoice evermore," and to "rejoice in the Lord always?" Let me be the first to say, that is a really bad counseling approach! Nevertheless, those Bible verses are still there. Is there something wrong when you are not rejoicing in the Lord always? If joy is a fruit of the Spirit, then you should be happy all the time, right? Philippians 4:4 does say, *"Rejoice in the Lord always. Again, I will say rejoice!"* In this same letter Paul also talks about *"sorrow upon sorrow"* (2:27), so perhaps this concept is brought into context in 4:7, *"And the peace of God, which surpasses all understanding, will guard your hearts and minds through Christ Jesus."*

How can you experience pain and joy at the same time? I picture a mom and dad, walking into the airport with their 19-year-old son. He graduated high school as a star athlete and at the top of his class with several scholarship offerings. However, he has decided to join the military and serve his great country. He has impressively completed basic training and is now being deployed to serve in the United States Army in war-torn Afghanistan. As they hug their son and watch him walk away through the airport terminal, these parents' hearts swell with pride and joy as their handsome and impressive son walks away to bravely serve his country. And, at the very same time, the tears flow without restraint as he disappears into the crowd. They are fully aware this may be their last face-to-face conversation with him on this side of eternity. These dear parents are experiencing pain and joy at the same time.

Having the joy of the Lord is not a state of constant euphoria. Scripture hardly presents it that way. Life circumstances are real. But, so is the great work that Christ has done in the heart of every believer. And, so are the great promises of Christ regarding our future. *"Let not your heart be troubled; you believe in God, believe also in Me. In My Father's house are many mansions; if it were not so, I would have told you. I go to prepare a place for you. And if I go and prepare a place for you, I will come again and receive you to Myself, that where I am, there you may be also"* (John 14:1-3).

Joy and pain will be intermingled while sin plagues the beautiful world God made. One day we will experience the full revelation of perpetual joy. John the Revelator *"heard a loud voice from heaven saying, 'Behold, the tabernacle of God is with men, and He will dwell with them, and they shall be His people. God Himself will be with them and be their God. And God will wipe away every tear from their eyes; there shall be no more death, nor sorrow, nor crying. There shall be no more pain, for the former things have passed away"* (Revelation 21:3-4).

Therefore, the foundation for our joy is deeper than just being happy, happy people. Our joy is built on the confidence that God is the guaranteed victor, and we are the recipients of His victory. Paul tells you to *"rejoice evermore"* and *"rejoice in the Lord always"* because God is always on the throne. His victory is just a matter of time and *that* reality never changes.

CHAPTER 3

OPEN LINE OF COMMUNICATION

"Pray without ceasing." What is prayer? Prayer is the open line of communication between you and God. Much too often, I have been told, "Pastor, I do not know how to pray." To which I reply in kindness, "I do not believe you." You know how to talk to everyone else, how could you not talk to your Best Friend? Many who would say they do not know how to pray may actually be confused by some bad religion. Prayer is not based on your ability to correctly insert "thee" and "thou", nor is it based on your ability to pray like your favorite preacher, or even like the prayers you heard Granny pray when you were a child. With the utmost respect to the Lord's Prayer, give me the license of simple practicality for just a moment. How do you talk to your spouse? How do you talk to your Momma? Your best friend? It is an open line of communication. Your focus is not to pray like Reverend SuperPreacher. Yes, he can pray for an hour and he is really impressive and all that, but his prayer life is not your prayer life. We want to know that we have an open line of communication with the Lord. When we pray, we can talk to the Lord like He is our best friend. You know why we can do that? Because He is. Tell Him everything. The more you pray the more that you want to pray. Prayer is a developed communication. It is developed as our own vocabulary. It is just like the developed communication you have with your spouse.

I remember the first date my wife, Tresa, and I had in November 1987. We both were so nervous, the conversation was very light and somewhat nerve-racking while we tried to think of something to say, and then hoped it was said the right way. But with time and trust, the more we talked, the more we had to talk about. The more we communicated, the more we could communicate. Fast-forward 30 years, with all of our life experiences, and the lifetime of memories, and a committed and devoted love from the deepest parts of heart; each day is filled with conversation on a personal level unknown to us back then. This relationship, based on time and trust, has given us the ability to communicate personally and intimately. As I learned Tresa's voice, the more I knew what she said when she said it. Over time, we learn that what your spouse says may not always be what he/she means. As young men, we thought that when she said, "That's fine," it meant that it was okay. Over time we discover that is not always true. Sometimes when she says, "That's fine," you know it is anything but fine! When she says, "It does not matter," you know that usually it really does matter! Sometimes, she does not have to say anything but I know loud and clear that all is not well. Likewise, we have learned that one word or even one look can speak volumes about love, or care, or passion that goes far beyond hours of conversation. You did not know that when you first met; it comes from a developed relationship of love, with time and trust.

It's the same thing in our relationship with God. In the beginning, sometimes we miss it. God speaks to our heart, but we are too young (spiritually immature) to figure it out. But the more that you talk to Him and the more He talks to you, the more you know what He is saying to you. A powerful open line of communication is developed. It's deeper than a prayer meeting. It's much deeper than a word of prophecy. His Words speak specifically to your heart about your daily life. The Spirit provides quiet but insistent direction in your walk with Christ. And, in those moments of uncertainty, *"…the Spirit also helps in our weaknesses. For we do not know what we should pray for as we ought, but the Spirit Himself makes intercession for us with groaning which cannot be uttered"* (Romans 8:26). Other than the amazing miracle of being able to pray in God's perfect will, you have the added bonus of praying far above Satan's knowledge — he has no clue what you are saying. It is the private line of communication between you and the Lord, where nothing is off-limits.

Another prayer excuse I hear is, "I do not have time to pray." What?? You do not have time to not pray! This excuse is both foolish and dangerous. If we have time to watch television, we have time to pray. If we have time to scroll through Facebook, then we have time to pray. If we have time for Twitter, Instagram, YouTube, and more, then we have time to pray. Prayer is essential, because when we pray about every situation in our life, then our lives are seen against the backdrop of God's goodness.

The well-known story of Daniel and his prayer life is much greater than his determination to pray in the face of a death threat. The miracle from Daniel chapter 6 goes beyond Daniel's commitment to a prayer life. The miracle is that King Darius became a believer in the Lord God Jehovah. The king issued a decree that the entire nation of Persia should give honor to "the God of Daniel." And, the miracle continues as seen in the great revelations Daniel received later in life, due in no small part to a faith-filled, consistent prayer life. Prayer caused him to see every situation against the backdrop of the Word.

One of the best life lessons that God ever taught me is this — God always proves His people. I do not have to prove anything to anyone. I do not have to impress you with my church growth concepts, my preaching skills or my great anything else. Any success we achieve in or out of the church is best created with a faith-filled, consistent prayer life. Our God is a prayer-answering God. Spiritual success is achieved when we pray without ceasing. When we pray, we do not see problems; we see the presence of the Lord. When we pray, we do not see the lion, we see the victory. When we pray, we do not see the fire, we see the Fourth Man in the fire. When we pray, we do not see the storm, we hear the Lord's voice saying to the raging storm, "Hush, peace be still." When we pray, we do not see the enemy; we see the table He has prepared for us in the presence of our enemies.

Against the backdrop of His Word, though you may see lack, when you pray you will hear *"I will supply all your need according to My riches in glory"* (Philippians 4:19). Your doctor's report may be negative, but when you pray you will hear, *"By His stripes you were healed"* (1 Peter 2:24). Prayer changes our focus from the natural to the supernatural. Just speaking Bible verses accomplish nothing. But when I speak the Word in prayer by faith, it must happen! Jesus was emphatic about this promise — *"Most assuredly, I say to you, whatever you ask the Father in My name He will give you"* (John 16:23). Not just a bunch of words — His Word in prayer, by faith, is done. In prayer, I can articulate the things that I believe for but cannot see right now. Prayer changes my focus from the natural to the supernatural.

THE FORCE OF PRAYER

Prayer drives out compromise. Prayer drives out carnality. Prayer drives out confusion. Prayer drives out foolishness. Prayer puts you in line with God's will. When Jesus knew it was time for Him to go to the cross, what did He do? He prayed. Imagine the overwhelming pressure of this one evening. This is the night that Judas will betray Him. This is the night that most of the disciples will run. This is the night that He will be left alone. This is the night that He goes to Pilot's hall. He knew and told His followers that He had come *"to do the will of the Father"* (John 5:30). It's one thing to say it, now it is time to fulfill it. This night of loneliness and pressure in a dark garden is not easy. It was a joy when He multiplied the loaves and the fishes, walked on water, and turned water into wine, but now? Now, the strongest of the soldiers are ready to beat His precious body. He knew what He was supposed to do, but there is little desire to submit to it. What did Jesus do? He prayed. He placed this most dynamic moment in the backdrop of God's will. *"O My Father, if it is possible, let this cup pass from Me; nevertheless, not as I will but as You will"* (Matthew 26:39).

After a quick and disappointing check on the disciples who accompanied Him, Jesus went back into the garden. To do what? Pray. And again, He prayed. Three specific times, under great duress, His response was to pray. What changed between verse 39 and verse 45 (*"Then He came to His disciples and said to them, 'Are you still sleeping and resting? Behold, the hour is at hand, and the Son of Man is being betrayed into the hands of sinners. Rise, let us be going. See, my betrayer is at hand."*)? He prayed until He saw this moment against the backdrop of the Father's Word. After the third time of prayer, He says, "Okay, let us be going. An hour ago, I was not ready but now I have it." How did that come? It was not because He suddenly became very brave. It was not because the planned events of the next day changed. It came because He prayed. As the elder saints in our little country church used to say, "He prayed until He prayed through." Pray until you get an answer. When you are having a problem and when you are being tempted, you pray until you can walk away, saying, "All is well now."

Even in His most personal and powerful moment, Jesus still took time to check on His men. He knows they did not get it. They are too spiritually immature. What was His admonition? *"Watch and pray, lest you enter into temptation. The spirit indeed is willing, but the flesh is weak"* (Matthew 26:41). Regrettably, this verse is now half-quoted and used to sheepishly excuse away our mistakes. "Well, Pastor, I know that I should not have done that, and I know that I should not have said that, but you know what the Bible says, 'The spirit is willing but the flesh is weak.'" Instead of using that verse to excuse ourselves from foolish mistakes, through prayer we can elevate our lives to victory with that same principle. The spirit is willing and powerful because we have a life of prayer, so our flesh is weak (it is not in control). The flesh has no control over our spirit man because we walk in the power of the Holy Ghost. When we watch and pray, our willing spirit has dominion over our weak flesh. Our spiritual eyes stay wide open through a consistent lifestyle of watching and praying.

One of the favorite "church-isms" of the 21st century is, "we're going to another level." It sounds exciting, it sounds promising, and it usually gets a positive response from the amen corner. I submit to you that going to another level is not necessarily a God thing, it is usually a personal thing. The foundation of spiritual progress and elevation is prayer. We love to praise God, but we cannot be so in love with the excitement of praise that we forget Who we are praising. I submit for your consideration that we are a generation that enjoys church more than we enjoy prayer. We enjoy preaching more than we enjoy prayer. We enjoy praise more than we enjoy prayer. Remember that Lucifer was in charge of worship in Heaven. He got so caught up in the worship that he thought it was his glory and not God's. Your praise and your worship are never to exalt you. Regardless of how pretty you sing, regardless of how amazing you can play, regardless of how many enjoy your gift, regardless of how electrifying the atmosphere is in the house — it is always all about Him, and it is never ever about us. It is difficult to be self-focused when we pray because prayer requires humility. James 4:10 says, *"Humble yourselves in the sight of the Lord, and He shall lift you up."* The humility of prayer states that our heart is open to God and His leadership. We do not know everything, and we do not have everything, and we cannot fix everything.

Prayer is a powerful thing, and the very concept of prayer will blow your mind if you really think about it. Prayer is you having a personal audience with the Lord God Jehovah, the creator and the ruler of the world and all that is in it. The very fact that the infinite God would even allow mortal man to speak to Him is unbelievably amazing.

Did you ever wonder why that out of all the things we do in church, our prayer time is one of the shortest parts of the service? We have a 45-minute music set, and then a 4.5 minute prayer time. Why? We have a limited prayer life. If you quickly run out of things to say to God, maybe you do not talk to Him very often enough. Most of us love to talk. You have been late for things because you were busy talking — a phone conversation, a break room conversation, a conversation with your spouse — but I wonder how many of us have been late for work or for a meeting because we got so caught up in prayer that we forgot the time?

ACTIVE LISTENING

I know we all do it, but it is really no fun to talk to yourself. We love to talk to other people. The reason we talk to other people is because we know they are listening and that they are engaged. When someone is actively listening, it motivates you to communicate. The main reason why people do not talk to God is because they are not really convinced that there is Someone on the other end actively listening and engaged. James 5:16 says, *"The effectual fervent prayer of a righteous man avails much,"* but your prayers will not be fervent unless you are convinced that God is listening.

Whether we believe it or not, God is always listening. Before the first word of prayer comes out of your mouth, God is listening. Regardless of whether you are right or wrong, God is listening. Regardless of whether you are weak or strong, God is listening. Regardless of whether you deserve blessing or correction, God is listening. *"The eyes of the Lord are over the righteous, and His ears are open unto their prayers"* (1 Peter 3:12). Yes, it goes on to say that *"His face is against them that do evil,"* but that does not mean that He is not listening.

When we walk outside of God's Word and the leadership of His Spirit, we distance ourselves from the glory of His presence. Yet, He is always listening. In your lowest moment, you are one prayer away from forgiveness; on your worst day, you are one prayer away from God's grace; when you spiritually fall flat on your face, you are one prayer away from your Father's hand reaching down and pulling you up out of your mess. And just because people are slow to forgive (and they have really long memories), it does not change the nature of the Lord. Your Bible says in Nehemiah 9:17 that the Lord is *"ready to pardon, gracious, and merciful, slow to anger, and of great kindness, and does not forsake us."*

CONFIDENT PRAYER

John said in 1 John 5:13, *"These things have I written unto you that believe on the name of the Son of God, that you may know that you have eternal life."* Do you know that you have eternal life through Jesus Christ our Lord? What is your confidence regarding your relationship with God? It is really simple — either you have eternal life in Christ or you do not. Read it again: "That you may KNOW that you have eternal life." There's no way to be a little bit saved. Either you are or you are not. Period. Quit rolling around in this perverted "greasy grace" doctrine of living like hell and hope you are going to heaven. You can **know** you are a child of God. Paul said in Philippians 3:10, *"That I may know Him, and the power of His resurrection, and the fellowship of His sufferings, being made conformable unto His death."* The fellowship of His suffering is not someone talking about you because you go to church. It is not someone making fun of your methods of worship. The suffering is when the carnal man is crucified so that the spirit man can be filled with the Holy Spirit of God. Romans 8:6 says, *"For to be carnally minded is death, but to spiritually minded is life and peace. Because the carnal mind is enmity against God, for it is not subject to the law of God, neither indeed can be. So then they that are in the flesh cannot please God."* But, verse 14 says *"for as many as are led by the Spirit of God, they are the Sons of God ... For we have received the Spirit of adoption, whereby we cry, 'Abba, Father.'"* We are in a relationship with God through Jesus Christ His Son and our Savior. So, yes, I can have an audience with God because He is my Daddy and I am His son. And, when I know that I have this relationship, I become sure of who I am and Who He is. I know Someone and I know some things! *"This is the confidence that we have in Him, that, if we ask anything according to His will, He hears us"* (1 John 5:14). The word 'confidence' comes from the Greek word *parrésia*, which means 'bold, plain and outspoken.' If you know you are saved, then you can be bold when it comes to your prayer life. If you know you are saved, then you can know without any reservation or hesitation that you have God's attention. And when you have a bold prayer life, not only do you have God's attention, but it will always get other people's attention. People who make fun of you for being "one of those Christians," will come to you when they get in a critical situation and ask you to pray for them. People who have blown off every invitation you have ever made to them to come to church will ask you for prayer when they have an emergency situation in their life. A bold prayer life says you know you can get in touch with God, any time, any where, and any place. You have confidence that God hears you!

Wherever you are, God is there. David said, *"If I ascend up into heaven, You are there; if I make my bed in hell, behold, You are there"* (Psalm 139:8). Jonah was lying in the guts of a great fish with seaweed wrapped around his head. And he said, *"I cried by reason of my affliction unto the Lord, and He heard me, out of the belly of hell I cried and He heard my voice"* (Jonah 2:2). You need to know that wherever you are, He is there. When you whisper the name of Jesus, He is there and He is listening.

HIS WILL

"This is the confidence that we have in Him, that, if we ask any thing according to His will, He hears us" (1 John 5:14). I believe the greatness of this promise has been clouded by four simple words: *"according to His will."* How do you know the will of God? How do you pray according to His will? Here is the answer — to pray according to His will is to pray His Word. His Word reveals His will. There is no will of God that is in contradiction to His Word. The Word of God is the Will of God explained. When you pray, you pray what it says. I know what I have a right to ask for based on what The Book says. If we do not know what it says about a specific need or situation in our life, we will not know how to pray effectively and correctly.

There is no way to be spiritually mature without a solid Word foundation. A solid Word foundation is established from Bible study and the teaching and preaching of God's Word. If we do not know the Bible, then we do not know how to pray. If we do not know how to pray, then we do not have communication with God. If we do not have communication, then we do not have a relationship. If we do not have a relationship, then we do not know Him. If we do not know Him, then we have no confidence that we have eternal life. When we do not know the will of God, we will spend years being led by the flesh instead of learning what we need to know. One hour of Bible study, one Sunday morning sermon, or one Wednesday night teaching could save us years of making dumb decisions. One Bible chapter a day coupled with a daily prayer life could save us years of living beneath our privileges as a child of God because we do not know how to pray His will for your life. We are often encouraged to "speak the Word" — what are we going to speak if we do not know what it says? We cannot just speak anything. If we go with just what feels good, that will lead to manipulation and witchcraft. Just anything will take us into seduction and mind-control. Just anything will take us into the world of positive thinking and if it feels good, then do it. We pray according to His will, and His will is His Word. Thankfully, when we pray fleshly, carnally-motivated, mind-inspired prayers, God typically does not give us what we ask for!

Your confidence in your relationship with God, your confidence in knowing His Word, and your confidence in the fact that He is listening is just as important as the asking. The confidence is what stirs the faith of the Word that you know. This gives us a greater understanding of Hebrews 4:14-16, *"Seeing then that we have a great high priest, that is passed into the heavens, Jesus the Son of God, let us hold fast our profession. For we have a high priest Who is touched with the feeling of our infirmities, but was in all points tempted like as we are, yet without sin. Let us therefore come boldly unto the throne of grace, that we obtain mercy, and find grace to help in time of need."* We do not receive anything when we waver. "Come boldly" is not arrogance, "come boldly" is confidence. Come boldly and then ask.

Asking is not just faith, asking is a type of praise. How is that? Because you never ask anything of anyone unless you believe they have it. The fact that I ask God for it indicates that I believe He has it. Whether He does it or not, I do not yet know. But when I believe He can do it then I will ask Him to do it. Believing that He is able is praising Him for His ability. Three young Hebrew men named Shadrach, Meshach, and Abednego, said to King Nebuchadnezzar, *"we do not have to defend ourselves in this matter; our God Whom we serve is able to deliver us from the burning fiery furnace, and He will deliver us from your hand, O king; but if not, let it be known unto you, o king, that we do not serve your gods, nor will we worship the golden image which you have set up"* (Daniel 3:16-18). "But if not" is not a lack of faith, it is the acknowledgment of God's sovereignty. What God does about our situation is up to Him, but we do know that He is able!

ASK

So what do we do? Ask. Which may cause you to say, how do we ask? What is the best way to pray? You can bow on your knees or you can stand up; you can close your eyes or you can look up; you can pray while you work, you can pray silently, you can pray out loud, you can cry and pray. You can get so emotional that they will think you are drunk (read the story of Hannah in 1 Samuel chapter one). You can whisper a prayer so quietly that the person next to you does not even know you are praying. The methods of prayer are as individual as there are people — you pray as His Word has spoken to you and you pray who you are. It is nobody's business to tell you how to pray. You have a personal relationship with your heavenly Father; who am I to tell you how to talk to your Daddy? God does not focus on the method, His focus is on who is saying it. There is nothing that can stop God from hearing your prayer. *"The Lord's hand is not shortened, that it cannot save; neither his ear heavy, that He cannot hear"* (Isaiah 59:1). God can hear you, any way you say it, any time you say it, and He can reach you anywhere you are.

Each one of us must have a personal prayer life, and I am also a supporter of public prayer. I am a supporter of having prayer in the courthouse, on the football field, and in the classroom. But if you think about it, when people say "they took prayer out of school," that's really not true.

How can you take prayer out of anything? We cannot be prevented from praying! They may stop us from praying out loud, but no one can stop us from praying. Sew our lips together or throw us in jail — that does not stop us from praying. Our prayer life is not dependent on the decisions of the Supreme Court justices. The Apostle John was exiled to the Isle of Patmos, but he prayed in the Spirit on the Lord's Day, and God revealed to him the mysteries of the end of the age (The Book of Revelation). They put Paul in prison, but he prayed in the Spirit and he was caught away to the third heaven, seeing and hearing revelations of the Godhead that he was never permitted to reveal (2 Corinthians 12). They put Paul and Silas in prison, beat them and threatened their lives. At midnight they began to pray in the Spirit, and their jail cell turned into a soul-saving station under the power of the Holy Ghost (Acts 16). You absolutely cannot stop a man or woman of God from reaching the ear and the arm of God. When you say the name of Jesus — if you whisper it, cry it, scream it, or just say it in your mind — all of Heaven stands at attention, angels are dispatched on your behalf, and *"whatever things you ask when you pray, believe that you receive them, and you will have them"* (Mark 11:24).

If someone says they do not know how to pray, it may be because they are focused on the method and not the Master. David said, *"O LORD, You have searched me and known me. You know my sitting down and my rising up; You understand my thought afar off. You comprehend my path and my lying down, and are acquainted with all my ways. For there is not a word on my tongue, but behold, O LORD, You know it altogether"* (Psalm 139:1-4). In reality, while you are trying to figure out what to say, the Lord already knows what you are really thinking. Before it comes out of your mouth, He already knows what every word is going to be.

CONFIDENT PRAYER

Just because He hears you right now, does not mean you will get the answer you want right now. Did you ever ask your parents a question, and they did not answer? And you ask again, and maybe you ask again. And this is what you finally get back: "I heard you the first time." My dad was a little slow in giving me an answer sometimes because he believed that whatever he said is what he meant. He did not change his mind. My daddy believed that if he said, "No," and then he said, "Yes," that he had just told a lie. Sometimes he weighed out the matter to make sure he got it right the first time. Sometimes he waited to make for sure that I understood the importance of obedience and submission. Your Daddy knows what you need better than you do. How many things did I want so badly, but Daddy said no because it wasn't what I needed? How many places did I want to go, but Mom said no because I did not have any business going there? *"We have confidence that He hears us."* Do not think just because you are not seeing action that God is not moving on your behalf. You do not have to see the angels to have faith that they are working on your behalf. You do not have to know the mind of God to still know that He sometimes says, *"You have need of patience"* (Hebrews 10:36).

Our confidence does not rest on seeing immediate results — He is not a microwave God. Our confidence does not rest on having it your way — He is not a Burger King God. Our confidence rests in the fact that He is listening, and not only that He is listening, but our confidence is wrapped up in Romans 8:28 — *"And we know that all things work together for good to them that love God, to them who are the called according to His purpose."* This is where our enemy would like to convince us that we cannot get God's attention. We buy into that belief when we say things like, "I've gotta get a-hold of God." In effect, the devil wants us to think that God does not really love us. He will bring up our past, accuse us of failures or weaknesses, and try to convince us that we do not have enough faith. It is all a lie. It's a smoke screen, a deception.

Perhaps your bills are bigger than your paycheck, but we have this confidence that He hears us. Maybe the cancer is still present, but we have this confidence that He hears us. Even though your son is still in jail, we have this confidence that He hears us. It may be true that they are all talking about you, but we have this confidence that He hears us. You are sure that you have a call of God on your life, though it seems as if there are no open doors of ministry for you right now, but we have this confidence that He hears us.

Here is what we find in the dictionary for 'confidence':
- the belief that you can rely on someone or something.
- the state of feeling certain about the truth of something.
- a full trust.

We do not pray to win God's favor; we pray in God's favor. When we pray, we must have complete trust that we are covered by God's grace right now. God is on our side. You cannot win the favor of God; He already loves you with an everlasting love. How can you try to "get a-hold of God" when He is everywhere all at the same time? How do you try to find Him when His Spirit lives in you? *"The ways of man are before the eyes of the Lord, and He ponders all his paths"* (Proverbs 5:21).

Even though the Apostle Paul was a great man of God who wrote more of the New Testament than any other apostle, Paul says in 2 Corinthians 12:7 that *"a thorn in the flesh was given to me; a messenger of Satan to buffet me."* He says in verse 8, *"I pleaded with the Lord three times that it might depart from me."* Why did he pray three times? Because the first two times, God did not say anything. Paul prayed; nothing happened. Finally, on the third time, Paul heard the Word of the Lord — *"My grace is sufficient for thee, for my strength is made perfect in weakness."* Whatever Paul's thorn in the flesh was, God received more glory with Paul having the problem that He would have if He took Paul's problem away. Was Paul disappointed? Did Paul give up? Did Paul blame God, blame the preacher, blame the church, blame his momma? No, Paul picked up his pen, and wrote, *"we glory in tribulations, knowing that tribulation worketh patience, and patience, experience, and experience, hope; and hope maketh not ashamed, because the love of God is shed abroad in our hearts by the Holy Ghost which is given unto us"* (Romans 5:3-5, KJV).

PRAYER LESSONS

Jesus' main role while He walked in His earthly ministry was that of the teacher. He was often called Rabbi. No matter what is going on in your life, He is always teaching. The Lord will not pull you out of the middle of class if there is still instruction going on. And, school is not just about teaching. If there is no learning, then the teaching is in vain. A good teacher knows how to give information, but he also knows how to help you receive information. Knowledge is no good unless you know how to apply it. You can have a head full of knowledge, but if you do not know what to do with the knowledge, you are still a fool. In the school of life, how will we learn patience if we never learn how to wait? How will we learn about miracles if we have never been in an impossible situation? How will we learn to trust God if we have never stood in a place of no escape? Can we still trust God when He is not talking? His grace will take us through what we think we cannot take. His grace will carry us through what we never thought we could go through. His grace will help us endure things that we never thought we could endure.

You thought you were going to lose your mind, but you did not. You thought you were going crazy, but you have not. You thought about giving up, but you just would not. You thought you could not stand it, but you stood it. How did you do that? Because you had confidence that He hears you!

As the old saying goes, "Life happens." Stop throwing a fit, stop having a temper tantrum, stop whining, stop blaming the preacher, and stop changing churches. Let Isaiah 40:31 settle your heart: *"They that wait upon the Lord shall renew their strength; they shall mount up with wings as eagles, they shall run, and not be weary, and they shall walk, and not faint."* He may not come when you want Him, but He'll be there right on time! Whatever God has promised you, it shall come to pass. David said, *"I waited patiently for the Lord, and He inclined unto me, and heard my cry"* (Psalm 40:1). Jonah was in the belly of the whale for three days, but God heard his cry, and he came out preaching the Word and Nineveh was saved. Ezekiel was in the valley of dry bones, and the Bible says, *"They were very dry."* At the appointed time God heard his prophetic cry and the bones lived again (Ezekiel 37). Jeremiah was in a pit up to his chest in filth, but God heard his cry and he came out still preaching the Word (Jeremiah 38). Blind Bartimaeus sat by the wayside begging for years. When Jesus came by, the old blind man said, "Jesus, thou Son of David, have mercy on me." He did not get an answer right away and the church folk tried to shut him up to no avail. *"And many charged him that he should hold his peace; but he cried the more a great deal, 'Thou Son of David, have mercy on me.' And Jesus stood still, and commanded him to be called. And they call the blind man, saying unto him, 'Be of good comfort; He calleth thee.' And he, casting away his garment, rose, and came to Jesus. And Jesus said, 'What will you that I should do unto thee?' The blind man said unto him, 'Lord, that I might receive my sight.' And Jesus said unto him, 'Go thy way; thy faith hath made thee whole.' And immediately he received his sight, and followed Jesus in the way"* (Mark 10:48-52).

Our responsibility is to have confidence that He is listening. Our responsibility is to know that the answer will always be His will, and His will is in the Book. Our responsibility is to wait on the Lord because the timing of a thing is up to Him. Daniel fasted and prayed for 21 days, and at the appointed time, God revealed to him the mystery of the ages to come (Daniel 10). Samson spent years in the dungeon, working like an ox, but in the time of the great feast, when they thought it was time to party, God heard Samson say, "Lord, let me feel you one more time." God poured out on Samson the greatest power of his lifetime (Judges 16). Paul and Silas were thrown in jail for preaching Jesus Christ and Him crucified and for casting out devils in Jesus name. All day long they waited and they prayed. All evening long they waited and they prayed. But at midnight, their prayer shifted from "get me outta here" to a prayer of "this is a great place to praise the Lord." At midnight the jailhouse began to reel and rock, bringing the jailer out of the bed and ultimately bringing he and his family to their knees in a prayer of salvation. In the middle of the night, the apostles baptized the whole family (Acts 16)!

PRAYER OF FAITH

Do not kill your miracle with a doubting mouth. You receive your miracle with your prayer of faith. Remember that God is on your side. *"And this is the confidence that we have in Him, that if we ask anything...."* The Bible says "any thing." If it is a thing, God can do it. If it is a thing, God can fix it. If it is a thing, God can heal it. If it is has a name, I know the Name that is above every name. At the Name of Jesus, everything has to bow. He is bigger than cancer, bigger than diabetes, bigger than debt, bigger than depression, and bigger than divorce. The name of Jesus is bigger than all of the names of every sickness, infirmity, and disease. The Name of Jesus is bigger than all the names of wickedness, hatred, strife, and racism. The Name of Jesus is bigger than all the names of any witch, false accuser, or false prophet. Any *thing* is no match for the King of Kings when you pray!

Whatever circumstances are being moved in your favor or whomever God is dealing with on your behalf, pray and believe in confidence — faith with boldness; faith with assurance. How can you be calm when your life is falling apart? How can you be calm when the doctor shakes his head and says, "There is nothing we can do?" How can you be calm when the tow truck pulls your car down the street? How can you be calm when your husband walks out the door and says, "I am not coming back!"? Here is your blessed assurance — you have this confidence that He hears you. After you have made your petitions known to God (Philippians 4:6), leave it in His hands. He knows when to do it, He knows how to do it, and He knows who to use. David said, *"Rest in the Lord, and wait patiently for him; fret not because of him who prospers in his way, because of the man who brings wicked devices to pass; cease from anger, and forsake wrath; fret not in any way to do evil. For evildoers shall be cut off, but those that wait upon the Lord, they shall inherit the earth. The steps of a good man are ordered by the Lord, and he shall delight in his way. Though he fall, he shall not be utterly cast down, for the Lord upholds him with His hand. I have been young, and now I am old; yet I have never seen the righteous forsaken,* nor his seed begging bread. He is ever merciful, and His seed is blessed" (Psalm 37:7-9, 23-26)!

Paul exhorted us to *"be anxious for nothing, but in everything by prayer and supplication, with thanksgiving, let your requests be made known unto God"* (Philippians 4:6). There are three things you do in this verse — Prayer (God conversations), supplication (asking and entreating), and thanksgiving (worship). To the church at Colossae, he similarly wrote, *"Continue earnestly in prayer, being vigilant in it with thanksgiving"* (Colossians 4:2). I know you praise God for what He has done; today, I want you to praise God for what He is going to do. How can you do that? We have this confidence that He hears us.

God is good. When things go wrong, He is good. When things are all right, He is good. In the storm, He is good. In the stillness, He is good. In the silence, He is good. God is good, all the time. And all the time, God is good.

"And Jesus said unto them, 'Have faith in God. For assuredly I say to you, whoever says to this mountain, 'Be removed and be cast into the sea,' and does not doubt in his heart, but believes that those things he says will be done, he will have whatever he says. Therefore, I say to you, whatever things you desire when you pray, believe that you receive them, and you will have them" (Mark 11:22-24). Prayer is not always loud or in some kind of an emotional outburst. Faith-filled prayer does not have to have an emotional element. Faith-filled prayer has a believing element. You can only receive to the capacity you believe. Do you believe that you are talking to God and He hears you? Jesus said we can move a mountain with mustard seed faith. He is not necessarily talking about a real mountain, although God can certainly do that. Faith is potent. The smallest of your part can receive the greatest of His part. If you need to move a literal mountain, go rent a backhoe and start digging. Why is that important to say? Do not waste spiritual time and energy on silly stuff. God does miracles — it is only a miracle when it is impossible for me. Are you believing for a job? Get out of the bed

(preferably before noon), take a shower, fix your hair, brush your teeth, type up a resume, and go ask for a job. That's what you can do. What you need that you cannot control is favor. Favor is what God will give you. God opens doors of opportunity when you are knocking. Your need is not so big that God cannot handle it. When I have a conviction about the mighty power of God, without any doubt in my heart, then the smallest seed of true faith will change the mightiest of situations.

PRAYER ASSIGNMENTS

Jesus said, *"Whatever things you desire...."* Desire is defined as "a strong feeling of wanting to have something or wishing for something to happen." The Bible says in Psalm 37:4, *"Delight yourself also in the Lord, and He shall give you the desires of your heart."* This does not mean that God is Santa Claus and will just give us anything we want. He is actually saying, "He will put His desires in your heart." If you go back to the original Hebrew for the word "give," you will find the word "Qal." A more specific translation of the word 'give' ('Qal') is "assign." So let's try that again — "Delight yourself in the Lord, and He will assign (appoint, designate) to you His desires in your heart." God assigns your desires. Think about it — when you become a born-again believer, the things you desire change. What you used to chase after, you are no longer interested in. Why? God changed your desires. Your interests change, your dreams change, your likes and wants change. Why? There has been a change! You are now led by the Spirit and not your carnal mind. You used to be selfish, now you are very generous. You used to run around, now you are faithful. You used to be a drunk, now you are sober. A new desire has been designated in your life. When I delight in the things of God, He makes assignments in my heart that actually make it delightful to live for God.

It is much easier to have faith when we have a clear understanding of God's plan, purpose, and preference for our lives. These are the desires of God assigned in our heart! Which leads us to the next question: How can we know God's plan, purpose, and preference? Go to 1 Corinthians 2:9-12. *"Eye has not seen, nor ear heard, neither have entered into the heart of man, the things which God has prepared for them that love Him. But God has revealed them unto us by His Spirit; for the Spirit searches all things, yes, the deep things of God. For what man knows the things of a man, except the spirit of man which is in him? Even so the things of God knows no man, but the Spirit of God. Now we have received, not the spirit of the world, but the spirit which is of God; that we might know the things that are freely give to us of God."* This ties together beautifully! God makes designations in our heart of His plan, purpose, and preference (His desires become our desires), and the more that we delight in Him, the more He reveals the greater things of our future. We have not seen it, we have not heard about it, we have not even imagined it, but as we pray, the Spirit gives us previews of His future plans for us! Now, Romans 8:16 brings on a clearer meaning — *"the Spirit bears witness with our spirit"* — because your spirit has a whole new perspective. Your spirit has seen the previews, and your focus becomes what He has for you. You have not seen it or heard it nor has it entered your mind yet. While you are praying, the Spirit of God will deposit something greater into your spirit, and your desire changes to receive what His desire is for you to have!

In Numbers chapter 13, Moses sent 12 spies into Canaan to check it out. Moses said, "Bring us back a preview." I consider this a lack of faith moment for Moses. Moses said, "See the land, what it is; and how many people dwell there, and whether they are strong or weak, and what kind of land it is, good or bad, and how big are the cities." But God had already given Moses all of the preview that he needed to know all the way back in Exodus 3:7. *"And the Lord said, 'I have surely seen the affliction of my people which are in Egypt, and have heard their cry by reason of their taskmasters, for I know their sorrows; and I am come down to deliver them out of the hand of the Egyptians, and to bring them up out of that land unto a good land, a large place; unto a land flowing with milk and honey."* Moses, why are you sending spies to check out what God has already told you is yours? You do not need spies; you need to possess what you have been shown!

Now, far be it from me to challenge this great patriarch of God. But this concept is the same for us today when we do not pray — we become dependent on flesh. The reason we become dependent on flesh is that there is no fresh revelation. The reason there is no fresh revelation is that our desires are no longer His desires. The reason there is a desire shift back to the old way of living is that there is no revelation from the Spirit. The reason there is no revelation from the Spirit is that there is no fullness of the Spirit! How can we receive revelation from Him with whom we are out of fellowship?

Previews are powerful things. We base a decision on whether or not we will spend $10 on a movie ticket and $20 dollars on a bag of popcorn on the preview. A 90-second highlight reel is all we need to make a decision. We see the preview, we receive the information they want us to have, and then we make a determination. God has not shown me everything about my future, but I have seen the previews, and I have decided that "as for me and my house, we are going to serve the Lord!" I have not received my miracle yet, but He has shown me the previews, and I have decided that He is well able to supply all of my needs according to His riches in glory! I have not received my breakthrough yet, but He has shown me the previews, and I have decided that if God be for me, who can be against me? I may be broke today, but I have seen the previews, and I have decided that He is able to do exceedingly, abundantly above all that I can ask or think. The Holy Ghost is the Master of the preview. The preview shows you things to come. Your desires become the things of your future and not the old fleshly desires of the man you have already crucified at the altar and buried in water baptism.

"Whatever you desire when you pray" is not talking to the carnal desires of the flesh. If your prayer life is always dealing with flesh, then try praying like this: "Lord, extract the desires of the carnal mind and implant the desires of the Spirit in my heart." Let me make that even easier: "Lord, change my passion." If you have a passion for it, you will not stop until you receive it. David said in Psalm 63:1, *"O God, You are my God, early will I seek You; my soul thirsts for You, my flesh longs for You in a dry and thirsty land, where there is no water; to see your power and your glory...."* Stop praying words; ask God to give you a passion for His Word. When He assigns a Word in your heart, pursue it, run after it, live for it, and be willing to die for it. Jacob said, *"I will not let you go, until you bless me"* (Genesis 32:26)! When you have a passion for a thing, and you know it is a God-thing, then that is confirmation to you that the Holy Ghost has revealed it to you. If the Holy Ghost has revealed it to you, then you know it is yours! It is your intensity about it that gives you the willingness to pray; not words, but fervent prayer. James said that *"the effectual fervent prayer of a righteous man avails much"* (James 5:16)!

SEEING AND HEARING

When you pray, believe that you have received it, and you shall have it. "Well, all I see is drought." Yes, but you hear the sound of rain. What you see is temporary and carnal; what you hear is eternal and spiritual. That is why Elijah kept telling Gehazi to go look again (1 Kings 18:41). No rain for 3-1/2 years, but Elijah heard something. The drought has invaded the land. Livestock is dead and dying. People are dead and dying. There's nothing but death and dust as far as the eye can see. There has not been rain for so long that they have almost forgotten what rain looks like. But, the prophet of God heard something. *"I hear the sound of an abundance of rain."* Look at verse 43 — *"Gehazi looked out toward the sea* (he went to a place where he could see as far as could be seen by the human eye) *and there was nothing."* Elijah said, "Look again." Gehazi said, "There is nothing." "Look again." "Nothing." "Look again." Seven times of this back and forth. Seven times of seeing and hearing. While Gehazi is making trips back and forth to the edge of the mountain, Elijah has his face between his knees. Praying. When you have heard something, stop looking at the current condition and start speaking the prophetic word of revelation. Speak His will (His Word), because His desire has suddenly become your desire. Now, verse 44 — *"And it came to pass at the seventh time, that he said, 'Behold, there arises a little cloud out of the sea, like a man's hand.' And Elijah said, 'Go up and say to Ahab, 'Prepare your chariot, and get off this mountain, before the rain stops you.' And it came to pass in the mean while, that the heaven was black with clouds and wind, and there was a great rain....*" Here is a perfect place for Mark 11:24 one more time:"*Whatever you desire, when you pray, believe that you receive them and you shall have them.*" What you receive in your spirit will reject every negative voice that says you will never have it. You keep praying until you see the thing happen in your life. Your ability to believe that you receive it is what makes you able to have it. As a matter of fact, you get it before you get it. You have already received it before you receive it!

"What do I ask God to do?" Let me answer that with this: The greatest things of God are never received intellectually, they are received by faith. Here's Mark 11:24 one more time, "*Whatever things you desire, when you pray, believe that you receive them, and you shall have them.*" Your grain of mustard seed faith is absolutely sufficient to move mountains of obstacles, hindrances, and demonic plans, and receive every plan, purpose, and preference ever revealed to you by His Spirit.

REVELATION

There are three parts of a person — body, soul, and spirit. In our spirit we have God-consciousness, in our soul we have self-consciousness, and in our body we have world-consciousness. Your body gives you the ability to be able to live in the world and to have an awareness of natural things. Your soul gives you self-consciousness (your mind). In your soul, you have memories, affections, desires, and passions. What is often referred to as "spiritual warfare" takes place in the mind, and any dysfunctions in your life are generally in the soul (your mind). This is self-consciousness — you know who you are, where you are, and what is going on around you. If you lose your mind, you can be here and not know you are here. The body is alive, but you do not know it. That is what we mean when we say, "he is unconscious." The genesis of most of the things we do is in the soul realm, and that is where the enemy fights us. It is with your mind that you purpose to serve the Lord. *"When I would do good, evil is present with me. For I delight in the law of God after the inward man. But I see another law in my members, warring against the law of my mind, and bringing me into captivity to the law of sin which is in my members. O wretched man that I am! Who shall deliver me from the body of this death? I thank God through Jesus Christ our Lord. So then with the mind I myself serve the law of God, but with the flesh the law of sin"* (Romans 7:21-25). The enemy fights you in your mind, because most of your decisions, functions, and commands are made in your mind — what you think, your feelings, and your ideas. For some of us (perhaps for most of us at times), our mind is dysfunctional. Our mind wants to hold on to who we were, but our spirit has been born again. That creates warfare between the flesh and the spirit, and the battlefield is the mind. Some folks really struggle when they have trouble discerning between what the mind is saying and what God is saying.

When God gets ready to give us new revelation, He will usually bypass our mind and put it in our spirit. (If He put it in our mind, we would mess it up.) He puts revelation in our spirit (our "heart"). That is why we are encouraged to pray in the Spirit because we then bypass all the crazy stuff that is in the mind. This leads us back to praying in "God's will." He assigns His will in our spirit. *"He that speaks in an unknown tongue speaks not unto men, but unto God; no man understands him, howbeit, in the spirit he speaks mysteries"* (1 Corinthians 14:2). That is revelation — it is a mystery to your mind until your spirit receives it and believes it. Your spirit man cannot control your mind until it has received Divine revelation. (We will discuss the baptism in the Holy Ghost and praying in tongues in more detail in chapter six.)

A common church term, though not found in the Bible, is "spiritual warfare." What does that mean? *"For though we walk in the flesh* (that is the mind, not the fleshly body), *we do not war according to the flesh. For the weapons of our warfare are not carnal but mighty in God for pulling down strongholds, casting down imaginations, and every high thing* (pride) *that exalts itself against the knowledge of God, and bringing into captivity every thought to the obedience of Christ"* (2 Corinthians 10:3-5). When you pray in tongues, your mind does not know what is being said, so it is kicked out of the work that God is performing in your life. You are building up the power and authority of your inner man (Jude 20) so that as you move forward in your Divine assignment, the spirit is empowered enough to keep the soul (mind) under submission. You want your spirit man to be in charge because it has been born again — it has been delivered. Your mind is being delivered, but it is a process. Your body shall be delivered at the second coming of Christ or when you die in Christ. When God wants to bring revelation to you, He does not speak to what shall be delivered (your body), nor does He speak to what is being delivered (your mind). He speaks to what has already been delivered (your spirit). When you pray in the Spirit, you are praying from the part of you that has already been made complete — you are born again. Your body is not born again — you are just as old as you ever were. Your mind is not born again — one minute you are singing "Victory in Jesus" and the next minute you are wondering where you are going for lunch after church today. Our mind is goofy (sometimes almost schizophrenic!), but our spirit is complete. It is has been born again. The reason why God does the work of completion in our spirit is because of Who He is. Jesus said, *"God is Spirit; and those who worship Him must worship in spirit and truth"* (John 4:24). God knows our bodies are just a temple of clay and God knows how to handle our crazy minds. God knows the true identity of a man is his spirit, and since God is a Spirit, He does the work of deliverance in the part of us that is like Him. He communicates with the part of us that is like Him. He brings revelation to the part of us that is like Him.

Is there a purpose of praying with your understanding? Of course there is! It allows you to communicate with God on the level of your understanding so that you know that you have made your petitions known unto God. *"Do not worry about anything; instead, pray about everything. Tell God what you need, and thank Him for all He has done"* (Philippians 4:6, NLT). Another benefit of praying with your understanding is that you can vent all the thoughts, feelings, and ideas in your mind so that God can then replace the hurt and the confusion and the craziness with His healing and His peace that passes all understanding. When you talk it out, you get it out. *"Casting all your care upon Him, for He cares for you"* (1 Peter 5:7). Therefore, *"I will pray with the spirit, and I will pray with the understanding also"* (1 Corinthians 14:15). If you do not have a prayer language, ask for it. The baptism in the Holy Ghost is for you! *"If you then, being evil, know how to give good gifts unto your children, how much more shall your heavenly Father give the Holy Spirit to them that ask Him"* (Luke 11:13)? This gives you the ability to operate beyond the natural and operate in the Spirit.

UNITED PRAYER

"Praying always with all prayer and supplication in the Spirit, and watching thereunto with all perseverance and supplication for all saints" (Ephesians 6:18). The fact that we are loving praise and forsaking prayer is killing the power and effectiveness of the church. We have become world entertainers instead of world changers. We are admonished to pray daily and pray in every way, as there is more than one kind of prayer. We pray with the Spirit AND we pray with the understanding. Our effectiveness or the lack thereof is not just because we have limited prayer, but that our prayer is limited to just us. The Bible plainly tells us in this text, and even more plainly in James 5:16, to *"pray one for another."* Furthermore, it tells us to pray for our enemies. Jesus said to *"love your enemies, bless them that curse you, do good to them that hate you, and pray for them that despitefully use you, and persecute you ... that you may be the children of your Father which is in Heaven"* (Matthew 5:44-45). Do not pray about them, pray for them. This is where you get rid of anger, frustration, and hurt. When you pray for people, you will better understand the actions of the people you are praying for. You will not despise people that you understand. You will not be hurt by people that you understand. When you know why someone is the way that they are, it will not bother you when they do what

they do. When you have been praying for them, and you have an understanding of them, then you will not engage with other people when they start talking about them. Praying about people does not change anything. Gossiping about people does not change anything (and it is a sin). There are at least 32 verses in the Bible that specifically deal with gossip, and the one I like the best is Proverbs 26:20 in the New Living Translation: *"Fire goes out without wood, and quarrels disappear when gossip stops."* Do not use the old church-ism, "I love them, I just do not like their ways." No, you do not love them. Period. And, you will never love them until you pray for them. If you are unwilling to pray for someone to be blessed, and genuinely desire for a blessing in their life, then you are the one with the bitter spirit. You cannot be full of bitterness and full of the Holy Ghost at the same time. You cannot have *"blessing and cursing coming out of the same mouth"* (James 3:10).

Bitterness has a first cousin — his name is self-righteousness. Let's define both of these and I'll show you how closely they are related. Bitterness is "anger, disappointment, and resentment at being treated unfairly." Self-righteousness is "having an unfounded certainty of being totally correct and/or superior." How are these so related? The foundational thought is the same — "I'm right and you are wrong." How can I develop a relationship with God if I refuse to have a right relationship with his kids? If you are mean to my kids, you will not be my friend. You cannot be nice to me and not my family. I wonder if God may have a similar perspective.

Our victory is in our unity and our unity is in the Spirit. If my heart is not right, then I am not right. God does not need me; I need God. God by-passed a whole generation destined for the Promised Land because their hearts were not right. They had no faith, they complained all the time, they were constantly fighting against each other, and they were too busy being focused on themselves. They had no desire for the vision God had for them. It was the generation of "me, me, me." Hebrews 4:2 says that *"the word preached did not profit them, not being mixed with faith in them that heard it.*" God rose up a new generation and took them into the land that He had actually prepared for their parents. If I refuse to accept God's plan, preference, and purpose for my life, refuse to listen to what He has to say, and refuse to change when His Word hits my heart, then God will step over me and find someone who will. God will call you, but if you will not get the job done, He will find someone who will.

When Moses lost his true direction, hit the rock instead of speaking to it, lost control over his temper, and stopped being the humble leader God had called him to be, God snatched him out of the way. He held a private funeral service for Moses, buried him in a place that no one knows to this day, pulled Joshua up and out, and said, "Now, Joshua, Moses is dead. Get up, take these people, and go over to the other side" (Joshua 1:2). You might be all that in the eyes of man, but you are not so grand that God won't change you out. God may be developing my replacement right now!

What does all this have to do with spiritual prayer? Paul writes, *"For those who live according to the flesh set their minds on the things of the flesh, but those who live according to the Spirit, the things of the Spirit. For to be carnally minded is death, but to be spiritually minded is life and peace.... So then, those who are in the flesh cannot please God"* (Romans 8:5-6, 8). And, to his spiritual son Timothy, he declares, *"I desire therefore that the men pray everywhere, lifting up holy hands, without wrath and doubting"* (1 Timothy 2:8). You cannot pray effectively in anger, no more than you can pray effectively with doubt. Beware of the cancer of anger. *"Be not hasty in your spirit to be angry, for anger rests in the bosom of fools"* (Ecclesiastes 7:9). Regardless of what they did, what they said, or what they took from you, "it ain't worth it." Do not let anyone rob your right relationship with God. It is not worth it.

Remember what Jesus said in John 4:24: *"God is a Spirit, and they that worship Him must worship Him in spirit and in truth."* Therefore, God communicates Spirit to spirit. If you have anger in your spirit, then there is a wall that prevents God from speaking to you. Perhaps this now gives us a truer revelation of what Jesus meant in Matthew 15:8, when He said, *"This people draws nigh unto me with their mouth, and honor me with their lips, but their heart is far from me."* It does not matter what you say, it matters what is in your heart. Anger in your spirit is a dam that blocks holy communion with the Father through the Holy Ghost. I am not talking about violence. You can be very quiet and polite, but on the inside, you are sitting on years of anger and rage and disappointment and bitterness. Some folks are angry about stuff that happened years ago. Some folks are still angry at people who are now dead. You could be angry at people who have moved on with their lives, and do not even remember something that you have been thinking about at least once a week for the last ten years. Old hurts, anger, and anxiety become a cancer that affects our relationships with our children, our spouses, our church family … and it most definitely affects our relationship with God. Let it go — it is not worth it.

When we really want to have conversations with God, it is not so much about what comes out of our lips, it is our praying spirit. *"Behold, You desire truth in the inward parts, and in the hidden part You will make me to know wisdom. Purge me and I shall be clean; wash me, and I shall be whiter than snow. Make me hear joy and gladness, that the bones You have broken may rejoice"* (Psalm 51:6-8).

We cannot be worldly people with a church cover. God does not want an affair, He wants a wife. We cannot be satisfied to dance before a God that we do not talk to. "Lord, create in me a right spirit. Even when I run out of things to say, I want my spirit to keep on talking to Your Spirit, and I want my spirit to keep on hearing Your Spirit."

CHAPTER 4

GIVE THANKS IN EVERYTHING

"In everything give thanks, for this is the will of God in Christ Jesus concerning you".

I was born and raised in Kentucky and I am proud of it. Kentucky is a very diverse state in a lot of ways, including the climate. A running joke around here is, "If you don't like the weather, just wait 'til tomorrow." We know how it feels to have heat indices that are over 100 degrees in the summer. We know how it feels to have below zero temperatures with snow and ice in the winter. While I should be used to it, I am not a cold weather person. Period. During the winter, I always start my car several minutes before heading out, just to get it nice and warm. One morning this past winter, I followed my usual morning routine: get dressed, run outside to start the car with the heater on high, run back in the house to finish getting ready to leave. When I walked back out to get in my warm car to head out for the day, there was no car in the driveway. Now, that was a strange feeling! I looked around, hoping that no one was playing a trick on me early on this cold morning. No car, anywhere. After calling the police, the insurance company, the car rental company, and changing all the door locks on our house, my car was discovered later the same day just down the street, with nothing missing other than coins from the console.

Never during that day did I say, "My car has been stolen. Well, Praise the Lord!" But, I did not get mad at God because some rascal took my car around the neighborhood looking for quick cash. I was not happy that my car had been taken. It was mine and I wanted it back! But in the character of "in everything give thanks," my prayer had to be, "Father, I praise You that I have a car. You know where my car is, and I thank You that whether I get it back or that You help me get another car, I praise You that I have a car." We are not told to thank God **about** everything, we are told to give thanks **in** everything. Just go ahead and thank God. Why? 'Cause He's got you covered! We thank God in everything because in everything we can find a reason to praise God. Which leads us to my life verse: *"And we know that all things work together for good to them that love God, to them who are the called according to his purpose"* (Romans 8:28).

The spirit of dissatisfaction is a stronghold that the enemy uses to blind our spiritual vision, and it plays out in our local churches when you start hearing complaints. "That preacher is too loud," "he preaches too long," "the church is too big," "the music is too loud," "they start too early," "they start too late," "their services are too long," "I do not like the color of the carpet," on and on …. Just an observation — isn't it curious that you rarely hear church complaints from new Christians? The new babes in Christ love everyone in the church, they do not watch the clock during a worship service, and they love to volunteer without any regard for position or recognition. Over time, the love for worship, the Word, and fellowship is replaced with complaints and fault-finding. This is the heart of dissatisfaction. Dissatisfaction is a stronghold and an unsatisfied soul that needs attention. Chronic dissatisfaction is a big red flag that alerts us to an impending spiritual fall.

When we get dissatisfied, we start looking for something else. In 2015, General Motors spent $3.59 billion on advertising and Toyota spent $2.86 billion on advertising. Two auto manufacturers spent over $6 billion on commercials! Why? GM wants us to be dissatisfied with the old Cadillac, hoping that we will start checking out the new Cadillacs. Toyota wants us to be dissatisfied with the Ford, hoping they can persuade us to check out a new Toyota. Even though there is nothing wrong with the car that I drive every day, if they can cause me to be dissatisfied with it, I will start looking at my options. If they keep showing me how wonderful their latest models are, then I will become dissatisfied with something I already own and used to love!

The enemy does the same thing with a child of God. When he can get us to not like the Word, and not like the preaching, and not like the preacher, and not like the preacher's wife, and not like the temperature, and not like the location, and not like the color, and not like the volume, and on and on and on, then we will start looking for something else. A dissatisfied soul stops enjoying what it used to love and start looking for something else. When we see people that are frequently moved by the latest and greatest, never happy and never settled, we are seeing the work of the enemy. *"A double minded man is unstable in all of his ways"* (James 1:8, KJV). The enemy does not want the Church to be settled and fed; he brings dissatisfaction to control and manipulate.

In reality, the work of the Holy Spirit in our life is the work of transformation as we evolve from the sensory to the spiritual. It is a work in everyone's life as we seek to make Jesus Christ the Lord of our life. Before Jesus, everything is sensual. The senses (we call it the flesh) of our life are all about what we see, hear, feel, etc. And before Jesus, there is no restraint in us. We look at whatever is pleasing to the eye, we listen to whatever is enjoyable to the ear, and we go wherever we feel like going, to do whatever we feel like doing. In Christ, the spirit man is transformed, and the transformation then goes from the inside out. We no longer live to please the flesh, we live to please the Father. The Bible says in Romans 8:8, *"Those who are in the flesh cannot please God; but you are not in the flesh, but in the Spirit, if indeed the Spirit of God dwells in you."* And, Paul continues in Romans 12:1, *"I beseech you therefore, brethren, by the mercies of God, that you present your bodies a living sacrifice, holy, acceptable to God...."*

Anyone who praises God does so by faith. Faith identifies God above and beyond situational circumstances. Another way to say it is this: we praise God by the revelation of Who He is, and not by what we see with our eyes. In my spirit, I am already delivered although in my situation it appears I am still bound. In my spirit, I am already healed although in my situation I still feel sick. In my spirit, I am wealthy although in my situation I am broke. The revelation by faith for my future is greater than the naturally perceived circumstance of my now.

Therefore, we know that faith is an integral part of our praise. God's people live in this world yet out of the world at the same. (I am talking about being spiritual, not being strange.) Having said all that, anyone can praise God. As a matter of fact, the Bible says in Psalm 150:6, *"Let everything that has breath praise the Lord."* So, I do not have to be "in the spirit" to praise God. So what did Jesus mean when He said in John 4:23, that *"the true worshippers will worship the Father in spirit and in truth"?* I do not have to be in the Spirit to praise God, but I do have to be in the Spirit to worship God.

If I asked you to give God some praise, you could say, "Praise the Lord." But praise goes much deeper than just lip service. In reality, true praise begins with asking. For example, if you came to me and asked me for $10, I could do that. If you came to me and asked me for $100, I could do that. If you came to me and asked me for a million dollars, I could not meet that request, but it would actually be an honor that you would consider me even able to have that to give. You would not have asked if you had not thought it possible. What about walking into a hospital room where someone has terminal cancer? You have the nerve to open your mouth and say, "Lord, I ask you to heal them right now." How many people do you know that can heal them of cancer? I only know One! When you ask God for the impossible, praise has just begun! And here is the sweet thing — whatever you ask, He gives you more than you ask for because He is able to do exceeding abundantly above all that you ask or think!

No matter where you are in life, you give God the praise anyway — this is thanksgiving — *"in everything give thanks."* Did you ever go out of your way to do something nice for someone, and they acted like they did not even care? I will tell you one thing that does for me — it causes me to make sure I don't go out of my way again! Your praise confirms that you honor God as your provider. The Bible says, *"Oh, give thanks to the Lord, for He is good! For His mercy endures forever. And say, 'Save us, O God of our salvation; gather us together ... to give thanks to Your holy name, to triumph in Your praise.' Blessed be the Lord God of Israel from everlasting to everlasting! And all the people said, 'Amen!' and praised the Lord"* (1 Chronicles 16:34). The word "blessed" in verse 16 comes from the Hebrew word "berakah." It is found 331 times in the Bible, and it literally means "to be adored." What God is looking for is for someone with uninhibited adoration. God has been so good that you want to adore Him with praise and worship that comes out of your innermost being. That house you woke up in this morning? That was the goodness of God. The car you drive? I do not care if you are driving a '75 Pinto — God has been good to you. The clothes on your back, the shoes on your feet — God is a good God. "Berakah" — I adore you for the big things, and they are all big things! If it is all good, then I should have all praise. David said, *"I will bless the Lord at all times, and His praise shall continually be in my mouth"* (Psalm 34:1). The word "praise" comes from the Hebrew word "Halal," which means "to boast." Your God loves to be bragged on. When I brag about God, I get to boast about what He has done, and what He is going to do. I can brag on the Lord! As we often heard in testimony service, "He has been better to me than anyone else."

So, let me "halal" for just a moment! When I was lost, He saved me. When I was in bondage, He delivered me. When I was empty, He filled me. When I was sick, He healed me. When I was broke, He blessed me. When I lost my way, He found me. When I messed up, He restored me. When I failed Him, He restored me. When I was depressed, He gave me joy. When I was weeping, He gave me happiness. When I was in darkness, He was my light.

If we give thanks in everything, then we are blessing the Lord. When we bless the Lord, we walk in the assurance of satisfaction, knowing that wherever we are right now, we stand in God's will. When we are thankful all the time, we do not have the desire to complain. We do not complain because we know we are blessed. Had a rough day at work? Yes, but you have a job! Is your house a mess? Yes, but you have a place to live! Are your kids driving you crazy? Yes, but you have a family to love! Have you not been feeling well? Maybe so, but you are still alive! Chronic complaining may be a common pastime of many, but we must not let it infect us and affect our hearts. The Scriptures show us that Paul experienced many disappointments throughout his ministry, but he obviously learned to resist the spirit of dissatisfaction: *"… I have learned how to be content with whatever I have. I know how to live on almost nothing or with everything. I have learned the secret of living in every situation, whether it is with a full stomach or empty, with plenty or little. For I can do everything through Christ, Who gives me strength"* (Philippians 4:11-13, NLT).

THE SPIRIT OF DISSATISFACTION

From the beginning of Moses' life, the one thing that he always had on his side was his family. Miriam made sure that her baby brother got into the hands of Pharaoh's daughter, and essentially back into his own mother's bosom when all the other babies were being killed. Aaron boldly stood in the face of Pharaoh and was the mouthpiece for his brother, because Moses had some form of a speech impediment. Miriam led the sisters in a great shout of victory when the horse and rider of Egypt drowned in the great Red Sea. The Bible calls Miriam a prophetess, anointed to declare the mysteries of God to the people, and in Exodus 4:29, it was Aaron who *"spoke all the words which the Lord had spoken unto Moses, and did the signs in the sight of the people."*

Even though Moses had murmerers and complainers and the stress of leading some faithless Israelites on their journey through the wilderness, he always had the support of his big sister, Miriam the prophetess, and the powerful and eloquent big brother, Aaron, the anointed man of God. Even though they had some people issues along the way, the journey to the Promised Land carried on, until one day, something went terribly wrong. It was overheard that Miriam was talking about her baby brother. Why did Miriam go off on her brother, putting her mouth of criticism on him and sowing seeds of rebellion against the man of authority? Satan has instigated this time and time again. He loves to sow discord in homes, in marriages, in relationships, in businesses, and in the church. The enemy of our soul wants to derail the work of God in our lives. He wants us to compromise the anointing that is in our lives. And he does that by subtle deception that blinds our spiritual vision.

Numbers 12:1 says, *"Miriam and Aaron spoke against Moses ...."* Did you ever hear that in the church? "She's got on another new dress." "The pastor has on another new suit." "Did they just get a new car?" Miriam and Aaron were not only talking against their baby brother, but their God-appointed leader. The text says they were talking about him *"because of the Ethiopian woman whom he had married."* But, that was not the real issue. They really did not care that he had married a fine black woman. The problem was envy and jealousy. *"So they said, "Has the Lord indeed spoken only through Moses? Has He not spoken through us also"* (v.2)? What happened to cause Miriam to despise where she once had honor? Miriam became dissatisfied because she felt disrespected. She felt like the leadership team was not getting equal attention. It is the "What about me?" syndrome. They are always talking about Moses, what about me? I can preach, but they never ask me! I am an usher, but no one is bragging about me! I am a greeter and they see me before they see the pastor, but no one is looking at me! Miriam was saying, "Moses is getting all the attention." "Everyone is talking about how great and anointed Moses is, what about me? I come out here every week. I prophesy. I lead the people in praise and worship." Listen, Sister Miriam, if it were not for the Word of God and His divine appointment, you could not lead anyone in praise and worship!

There are consequences when the once thankful heart becomes jealous and envious. *"(Now the man Moses was very humble, more than all men who were on the face of the earth.) Suddenly the Lord said to Moses, Aaron, and Miriam, 'Come out, you three, to the tabernacle of meeting!' So the three came out. Then the Lord came down in the pillar of cloud and stood in the door of the tabernacle, and called Aaron and Miriam. And they both went forward. Then He said, 'Hear now My words: If there is a prophet among you, I, the Lord, make Myself known to him in a vision; I speak to him in a dream. Not so with My servant Moses; He is faithful in all My house. I speak with him face to face, even plainly, and not in dark sayings; and he sees the form of the Lord. Why then were you not afraid to speak against My servant Moses'"* (vs. 3-8)?

JEALOUSY AND ENVY

Envy is a jealous discontentment of another person's prosperity, good fortune, or favor that gives birth to covetousness. Jealousy and envy are destructive and are the symptoms of a life that is not thankful. Jealousy and envy often lie hidden behind a fake smile and big hug until there is a seemingly acceptable perceived issue to get offended about and then attack. Envy keeps your relationships from growing because when we are jealous we cannot be trusted. Jealousy and envy hurt innocent people, and often times the innocent are the same people that have our best interests at heart. Jealousy and envy diminish our ability to enjoy a wonderful and happy life because of an ungrateful attitude. Jealousy and envy grow into resentment.

The damages of jealousy and envy are seen throughout the Bible in some well-known relationships. Their tragic effects are seen in the lives of Cain and Abel, Joseph and his brothers, and Saul and David. Before the beginning of time (and of which we have experienced the pain of the greatest conflicts), we know the impact of jealousy and envy created in the heart of Lucifer against God.

We choose to have a thankful heart. We choose to receive deliverance from jealousy and envy. Deliverance is achieved through the conviction of our choices. *"Set your affection on things above, not on the things of the earth"* (Colossians 3:2). We choose which road we will travel by receiving God's Word, accepting the work of the Holy Spirit in our heart, and then taking responsibility for our own actions. When I focus on my life, I no longer want to focus on yours.

Deliverance from jealousy and envy is achieved by a consecrated commitment. *"Whatever you do, do it heartily, as to the Lord and not to men"* (Colossians 3:23). The approval of others is not required to be successful because people are not your source. God is your source. When you know that Jesus is Lord of all, and Jesus is Lord over all, then you can live and do everything as unto the Lord. Live to His glory and not for your own glory. You are not on the earth so others can say you did a good job, you are on the earth so God can be glorified with your life. You are what you are by the grace of God.

God is most concerned about His people and His plan for their lives. God will seek us out when we mess up. God will seek us out to bring us into His plan. God sought out David when he messed up with Bathsheba. God sought out Elijah when he wanted to die. God sought out Moses when he killed the Egyptian slave master. God sought out Jonah when he ran from the call of the Lord. God sought out Peter when he denied knowing the Lord. Even though Miriam was separated from her family while experiencing the pain of leprosy (Numbers 12:10), her isolation was only temporary for a time of repentance. The key to restoration, purpose, and power is repentance. God will not leave you in your mess. After seven days, Miriam was restored, and no one moved on without her. And, when they all moved together, they were able to come into a place of great victory. *"So Miriam was shut out of the camp seven days, and the people did not journey till Miriam was brought in again."* When we repent we will feel contrition. When we have a change of the mind we can become restored. When we become restored we can experience revival. In revival, we "give thanks in everything!"

CHAPTER 5

HEARTBURN

"Quench not the spirit." Growing up in what is often called Free Pentecostal churches, we would often hear someone say during a church service, "Don't quench the Spirit!" It was their way of encouraging the church folks to sing or testify or preach, or whatever you felt impressed to do during the worship service. But the word "quench" (Greek — *sbennymi*) typically refers "to extinguish," as in putting water on a fire. While it also means to suppress, I am sure that the attitude of reluctance is not our greatest hindrance to the presence of God in our services. Therefore, allow me to focus on the word *quench* as meaning "to extinguish." If you put water on a fire, what does it do? It puts it out — it is extinguished. One of the symbols or attributes of the Holy Ghost is fire. John, the forerunner of Jesus Christ, introduced the Holy Ghost in this manner: *"I indeed baptize you with water unto repentance, but He Who is coming after me is mightier than I, whose sandals I am not worthy to carry. He will baptize you with the Holy Spirit and fire. His winnowing fan is in His hand, and He will thoroughly clean out His threshing floor, and gather His wheat into the barn; but He will burn up the chaff with unquenchable fire"* (Matthew 3:11-12). And again, when Jesus baptized the church with the Holy Ghost, as recorded in the book of Acts: *"And when the day of Pentecost was fully come, they were all with one accord in one place. And suddenly there came a sound from heaven as of a rushing mighty wind, and it filled all the house where they were sitting. And there appeared unto them cloven tongues like as of fire, and it sat upon each of them. And they were all filled with the Holy Ghost, and began to speak with other tongues, as the Spirit gave them utterance"* (Acts 2:1-4, KJV).

When many Pentecostals/Charismatics see "the Holy Ghost" in the Bible, it is often understood to be the miraculous gifts of the Spirit, such as speaking in tongues, or prophesying, gifts of miracles, and so on. But, we understand if we use that interpretation, then it would be assumed that Paul is forbidding the exercise of these gifts from being hindered. Since Paul deals with that in the next verse, there is no reason to exclude the ordinary but still more valuable gifts of the Holy Ghost. What are those more valuable gifts of the Holy Ghost? Purity, holiness, and sanctification; these are "quenched" when sin is present. While the gifts of the Spirit may be more studied or desired, the spiritual wholeness of the believer is much more precious than the exercising of gifts by a believer.

Your Bible says very plainly to *"Pursue peace with all people, and holiness, without which no one will see the Lord; looking carefully lest anyone fall short of the grace of God; lest any root of bitterness springing up cause trouble, and by this many become defiled"* (Hebrews 12:14-15). He did not say you would not see the Lord without the gift of healing; he did say that without holiness you would not see the Lord. *"Quench not the Spirit"* has much more to do with allowing the Holy Ghost to do His purifying work in our hearts, and much less to do with how we participate in a church service.

THE FIRE HAS GONE OUT

Quite simply, sin diminishes the fire of the Holy Ghost. This was painfully learned by the failures of the high priest, Eli. *"And the child Samuel ministered unto the Lord before Eli. And the word of the Lord was precious in those days; there was no open vision. And it came to pass at that time, when Eli was laid down in his place, and his eyes began to wax dim, that he could not see; And ere the lamp of God went out in the temple of the Lord, where the ark of God was, and Samuel was laid down to sleep"* (1 Samuel 3:1-3, KJV). Some translations show the lamp being extinguished as simply turning it off for the evening, while other translations show it ran out of oil. The Scriptures often have a way of bringing a powerful spiritual connotation to a seemingly common moment. Since verse one plainly says that *"there was no open vision,"* it is apparent that there are deeper spiritual thoughts worth exploring. Why did the fire go out in the temple? Not just the evening lamp, but the fire of God that fell upon the altar, that gave visions and prophecies to the great men and women in the temple; that accompanied the precious Shekinah glory of the Lord in the holy place. Where is *that* fire? That fire was quenched because the kingdom of Israel and her leadership were filled with sin. The Shekinah (Biblical Hebrew: הניכש) is the English transliteration of a Hebrew word meaning the dwelling or settling of the divine presence of God.

When the fire of the Holy Ghost is extinguished, there is nothing left except the power of the enemy. Recently, someone actually said to me, "Well, I know I may not be serving God right now, but I am not serving the devil." Allow me to be frank — you are serving one or the other! Someone is the lord of your life, and that lord is who you designate to be in charge. *"Do you not know that to whom you present yourselves slaves to obey, you are that one's slaves whom you obey, whether of sin leading to death, or of obedience leading to righteousness"* (Romans 6:16). Someone is in charge of my life — God or Satan. Yes, I have free will, but my will is motivated by my heart which is directed by the lord of my heart. *"Therefore do not let sin reign in your mortal body, that you should obey it in its lusts. And do not present your members as instruments of unrighteousness to sin, but present yourselves to God as being alive from the dead, and your members as instruments of righteousness to God"* (Romans 6:12-13).

In the latter part of Eli's tenure, we see that his sons joined him in the administration of his duties at the temple, but not with God's approval. Because of the wicked ways of his sons, Hophni and Phinehas, God has warned Eli of judgment against his family and his administration. Unfortunately, *"because his sons made themselves vile, and he did not restrain them"* (1 Samuel 3:13), the judgment did come in the form of an invading Philistine army.

"So the Philistines fought, and Israel was defeated, and every man fled to his tent. There was a very great slaughter, and there fell of Israel thirty thousand foot soldiers. Also the ark of God was captured; and the two sons of Eli, Hophni and Phinehas, died.

"Then a man of Benjamin ran from the battle line the same day, and came to Shiloh with his clothes torn and dirt on his head. Now when he came, there was Eli, sitting on a seat by the wayside watching, for his heart trembled for the ark of God. And when the man came into the city and told it, all the city cried out. When Eli heard the noise of the outcry, he said, 'What does the sound of this tumult mean?' And the man came quickly and told Eli, '...Israel has fled before the Philistines, and there has been a great slaughter among the people. Also, your two sons, Hophni and Phinehas, are dead; and the ark of God has been captured.' Then it happened, when he made mention of the ark of God, that Eli fell off the seat backward by the side of the gate; and his neck was broken and he died, for the man was old and heavy. And he had judged Israel forty years.

"Now his daughter-in-law, Phinehas' wife, was with child, due to be delivered; and when she heard the news that the ark of God was captured, and that her father-in-law and her husband were dead, she bowed herself and gave birth, for her labor pains came upon her. Then she named the child Ichabod, saying, 'The glory has departed from Israel....'" (1 Samuel 4:10-14, 17-19, 21-22). When sin comes in, the presence of the Lord departs. Two gods can't live in the same house (1 Samuel chapter 5).

HOLY GHOST FIRE

Many in the Pentecostal/Charismatic and many other contemporary church circles have a history of being impressed by what we can see, what we feel, and what we hear. We focus on singing and shouting, energetic preaching, high emotions, and expressive worship. And the more we see, feel, and hear, correlates to how much we enjoyed the church service.

"Wow, we had church tonight! We churched it up!" And while I am all for an impactful spiritual encounter in God's house, and I embrace our traditional Pentecostal methods of worship, we must not overlook the fact that the Holy Ghost is not focused on our emotional experiences in a church service. *"Howbeit when He, the Spirit of truth, is come, He will guide you into all truth: for He shall not speak of Himself; but whatsoever He shall hear, that shall He speak: and He will shew you things to come"* (John 16:13, KJV). The Holy Ghost does not lead me to a shout, He leads me to the truth of God's Word. If I am living the life that correlates and parallels the Word of God, then I have every reason to rejoice. Or, as the saints of yesteryear would say, "I've got something to shout about."

The fire of the Holy Ghost does not bring an emotional church service. The fire of the Holy Ghost brings a separation between holiness and sin. *"Whose fan is in his hand, and he will throughly purge his floor, and gather his wheat into the garner; but he will burn up the chaff with unquenchable fire"* (Matthew 3:12, KJV). With God's people, there has to be a separation. John the Baptist never talked about shouting and dancing. The church that I proudly pastor, FaithPointe, is well known for our great music ministry. We are well known as a church of expressive praise and deep worship. While we are passionate about our individual and corporate expressions of worship, neither a shout, a dance, uplifted hands, nor tears of joy are the key components of spiritual power. If the fire of the Holy Ghost is not burning powerfully on the inside, then what happens on the outside is immaterial. If all we are about is on the outside — the shout, the rules, the dress code, the program — then we are nothing more than 21st century Pharisees, walking in the traditions of dead religion. We look good on the outside but dead on the inside. Such was Jesus' scathing indictment on the religious leaders of His day: *"Woe to you, scribes and Pharisees, hypocrites! For you are like whitewashed tombs which indeed appear beautiful outwardly, but inside are full of dead men's bones and all uncleanness"* (Matthew 23:37).

COMPLACENCY

Without the fire of the Holy Ghost, we become another Eli — our vision is dimmed and we become unaware of the enemy's activities around us. If the fire goes out, our spiritual eyes cannot see what is going on around us; and the enemy loves to work in the darkness. Darkness is not night, darkness is the absence of revelation and spiritual vision. This is where our enemy brings lies, deceit, and complacency that come with sin. Complacency brings compromise, compromise quenches the fire of the Holy Ghost, and now we are just walking in the same tradition that other people have done in the past.

The classic parable of the 10 virgins is a perfect example of the difference between religion and relationship. *"Then the kingdom of heaven shall be likened to ten virgins who took their lamps and went out to meet the bridegroom. Now five of them were wise, and five were foolish. Those who were foolish took their lamps and took no oil with them, but the wise took oil in their vessels with their lamps. But while the bridegroom was delayed, they all slumbered and slept.*

"And at midnight a cry was heard: 'Behold, the bridegroom is coming; go out to meet him!' Then all those virgins arose and trimmed their lamps. And the foolish said to the wise, 'Give us some of your oil, for our lamps are going out.' But the wise answered, saying, 'No, lest there should not be enough for us and you; but go rather to those who sell, and buy for yourselves.' And while they went to buy, the bridegroom came, and those who were ready went in with him to the wedding; and the door was shut.

"Afterward the other virgins came also, saying, 'Lord, Lord, open to us!' But he answered and said, 'Assuredly, I say to you, I do not know you.'

"Watch therefore, for you know neither the day nor the hour in which the Son of Man is coming" (Matthew 25:1-13).

Jesus described these 10 young ladies as "*... five of them were wise, and five were foolish*" (Matthew 25:2). How did Jesus distinguish between the two groups? It was not their title because all ten were virgins. We love to focus on our particular church label, the length of time we have been in church, or our methods of worship, styles, or baptism. Here is our question of relevance: is the fire of the Holy Ghost intensely burning in our lives right now?

When did the five foolish virgins realize that they did not have what they needed? They realized it when it was too late. At midnight the call came, "*the Bridegroom comes, go out to meet Him*" (Matthew 25:6). All ten heard the same sermon and all ten were members of the same church. Five got up and trimmed their lamps which were filled with oil. Their lamps are burning brightly and they are ready to go. They had kept their eyes wide open and were always prepared. When will Christ return for the church? I do not know. But whether He comes back today or 25 years from now, I want to be ready. I do not know when He is coming, but I do know this: "*The master of that servant will come on a day when he is not looking for him and at an hour that he is not aware of*" (Matthew 24:50). When the five that were foolish heard the call, they were unprepared and unaware of the time, even though they were all supposedly making plans for the same event.

It is interesting that the foolish asked the wise for resources. The wise make this point — "You must get it for yourself." This is why the believer must pray. The believer must know the Scriptures. The believer must live holy. That starts today. Delayed preparation is lack of preparation and lack of preparation brings disaster. "*And while they went to buy, the bridegroom came, and those who were ready went in with him to the wedding, and the door was shut. Afterward the other virgins came also, saying, "Lord, Lord, open to us! But he answered and said, 'Assuredly, I say to you, I do not know you.' Watch therefore, for you know neither the day nor the hour in which the Son of Man is coming*" (Matthew 25:10-13). I suspect one of the strongest and saddest statements to ever be heard would be, "I do not know you."

Prepare now. Secure your relationship now. Be aware of the times and seasons now. No one knows the day of the return of our Lord, but we know the *"times and seasons"* (1 Thessalonians 5:1). This is the time of the age (the dispensation of time), not chronological time. What should we be aware of regarding the times and seasons? What do our spiritual eyes see today?

"But know this, that in the last days perilous times will come. For men will be lovers of themselves, lovers of money, boasters, proud, blasphemers, disobedient to parents, unthankful, unholy, unloving, unforgiving, slanderers, without self-control, brutal, despisers of good, traitors, headstrong, haughty, lovers of pleasure rather than lovers of God, having a form of godliness but denying its power" (2 Timothy 3:1-5).

CHAPTER 6

THE PROPHETIC WORD

"Do not despise prophecies." Prophecy is the inspired declaration of the divine will and purpose of God. We are commanded to not depreciate the prophetic revelation nor despise the inspired instruction of His warnings. We thank God for grace, for mercy, and for all of the hundreds of blessings in the Word of God, but there are also some warnings, too. No matter our age, we can be childish. Without direction, we will do just about anything.

Do not despise prophecies; receive the instruction of the Lord. *"Speak these things, exhort, and rebuke with all authority. Let no one despise you"* (Titus 2:15). Speak the Word of God with exhortation, and rebuke the defiant and rebellious with a lifestyle above reproach in grace and authority. In the office of the prophet, the shepherds of God's people have been called to be a watcher of His house — the watchmen on the wall. The prophets exhort the people to stay under His covering, abide in His presence, walk in His grace, and live in His mercy. Prophecies give guidance and instruction. We must protect our hearts against self-reliance. As a believer, we must remember that there is always room to grow spiritually. Being a born-again believer will take us to Heaven. It does not mean that we have received full and complete knowledge of all spiritual concepts.

Consider a newborn baby. He has five fingers on each hand, five toes on each foot, and all of his internal organs function normally. He has everything he needs to be a fully functional human but he is not mature. There is a lot of "growing up" to do although he has all of the parts. If you are a child of God then you have all of the parts. Whether you have been a child of God for 30 years, 30 weeks, or 30 days, there is still some growing to do. The newborn baby starts out on milk. Without milk, he will die. However, after many months of growth, the milk that has given him life will not continue to sustain him. Eventually, without additional nutrition, that life-giving milk will begin to give stunted growth. For the new believer, we are encouraged *"as newborn babes, desire the pure milk of the Word, that you may grow thereby"* (1 Peter 2:2). With time and experience, deeper concepts and revelation of the Word must be received. *"For everyone who partakes only of milk is unskilled in the word of righteousness, for he is a babe"* (Hebrews 5:13). That revelation comes through receiving the prophetic utterances of the Lord, through His Word, by men and women anointed in the office of the prophet.

When the preaching of the Word pushes us to the next level of maturity, and we resist that exhortation (or even rebuke in the areas of strong resistance), that is the spirit of rebellion. Resistance to the prophetic Word can sound like this: "I do not like that preacher." "I do not want anyone to tell me how to live." "I can be a Christian without going to church." Here is a great opportunity for the enemy of our soul to feed rebellion and resistance. Such was the heart of Queen Jezebel against the prophet Samuel. This is often referred to as "the spirit of Jezebel," and it is not a reference to jewelry and makeup. "Jezebel" denotes rebellion against the Word of God. When King Ahab shared with his wife the great miracles that God showed His people on Mount Carmel, and how that Samuel had killed all of the false prophets of Baal, and how that all the prophets in her employ were dead, Jezebel sent the prophet of God a very dire warning, saying, *"So let the gods do to me, and more also, if I do not make your life as the life of one of them by tomorrow about this time"* (1 Kings 19:2). She cared only for the false prophecies that condoned sin which came from her hand-picked "prophets," not the truths of God or the miracles from God's hand. That is the "spirit of Jezebel." Sadly, that same resistance to the Word with signs following is alive and well today.

Paul's last exhortation to his associate and friend, Timothy, was to *"Preach the word! Be ready in season and out of season. Convince, rebuke, exhort, with all longsuffering and teaching. For the time will come when they will not endure sound doctrine…" (2 Timothy 4:2-3).* Every word of prophecy must be seasoned well with love and grace. When the heart of the prophet beats with compassion, the word will never be harsh or condemning, even in reproof. To suggest that the watchers of our soul cannot instruct us on how to live would be the same as saying that I cannot instruct my children. I told my kids what to do because I love them, not because I was mean or on an adult power trip. Over time our conversations changed but the heart of instruction and love did not. When my boys were toddlers, they were instructed at a primary level. When they turned 16, our discussions were at a very different level, but my heart of love for them had not changed. It is the same principle with our Christian maturity. The Word of God comes to exhort us, and over time it may even rebuke us if we continue in rebellion or foolishness, because we are not babies forever. The nursery is for a short period of time. Our spiritual success is in our spiritual maturity.

What happens when we are resistant to the mature "meat" of the Word? Paul answered that in his continued letter to Timothy: *"For the time will come when they will not endure sound doctrine, but according to their own desires, because they have itching ears, they will heap up for themselves teachers; and they will turn their ears away from the truth, and be turned aside to fables"* (2 Timothy 4:3-4). The truth of sound doctrine is forsaken for nice stories.

I know that many ministers have opportunities to share the Word with different people on many different spiritual levels. In our church, we have ministers and lay leaders who work with the homeless, the incarcerated, and those in recovery programs. The Gospel message they share on the streets, in the jails, and in recovery meetings will be at a different level than the pastoral message I share with our congregation on Sunday mornings. The beauty of the anointing is that God gives us the right Word at the right time for the right place in our walk with Him. Our responsibility is to *"lay aside all filthiness and overflow of wickedness, and receive with meekness the implanted word, which is able to save your souls"* (James 1:21). Only God truly knows what our spiritual maturity level is, and when the Word from the man or woman of God speaks to us, that is a great demonstration of His love toward us. A meek heart and an open spirit allow us to receive the Word. A meek heart and an open spirit cause us to receive the prophet of God with gladness. *"Obey those who rule over you, and be submissive, for they watch out for your souls, as those who must give account. Let them do so with joy and not with grief, for that would be unprofitable for you"* (Hebrews 13:17). How will we mature in the Word if we are resistant to the mature Word of instruction? Every born-again believer will give an account of his/her life when we stand before God. *"So then each of us shall give account of himself to God"* (Romans 14:12).

FAITHFUL MINISTRY

Every prophet of God will give an account of how he/she ministered to God's people. *"Be diligent to present yourself approved to God, a worker who does not need to be ashamed, rightly dividing the word of truth"* (2 Timothy 2:15). When I stand before God, I will give an account of my life in Christ, and I will give an account of my life as a pastor, a minister of the Word, an under-shepherd of His precious people. Every message I preached, every person that was in our pulpit, and every dollar that was spent shall be carefully matched with His Word. According to Matthew 12:36, every word we speak shall be weighed against His Word. While there may be a great level of responsibility inherent with serving in a position of leadership, it is not meant to be stress-filled and unproductive. I want to minister with joy. The unfaithful minister is not profitable to the local congregation.

The faithful minister maintains the standards of holiness. The faithful minister makes plain *"the goal for the prize of the upward call of God in Christ Jesus"* (Philippians 3:14). The faithful minister brings encouragement and compassion and proclaims the Word of God with passion and zeal. The blessing of the Lord rests upon the local church where the Word of God, the power of God, and the faith of God all reside in the same place. Let the Word of God be preached in its fullness! Let God be God in all of His fullness in our assemblies, and let us have an inner hunger for more — to hear more and to know more.

How important is the prophetic Word? *"How then shall they call on Him in whom they have not believed? And how shall they believe in Him of whom they have not heard? And how shall they hear without a preacher? And how shall they preach unless they are sent"* (Romans 10:14-15)?

Every promise to any believer is received by faith in God's Word. It begins with the plan of salvation, God's great promise to us: *"Whoever calls on the name of the Lord shall be saved"* (Joel 2:32, Romans 10:13). And thus, begins our development — growing *"in the grace and knowledge of our Lord and Savior Jesus Christ"* (2 Peter 3:18). A baby's body develops from newborn to adult. As believers, we are in the body of Christ (the Head), and through the ministry of the Word, under wise and anointed leadership, we grow up together (Ephesians 4:11-16).

Perhaps as a baby Christian, I am a fingernail in the body of Christ. I am humbled and forever grateful just to be in the body. But, what if I can "grow" from being the fingernail to becoming the finger, to becoming the hand, to the arm, to the shoulder? The shoulder can do what the fingernail could never do. Both are in the body, but one is more impactful, though not more important. In the body of Christ, no one is ever more important than the other, but some are more impactful. That is why there could be an inherent spiritual danger in being "saved, filled, and satisfied," and that in two ways. First, if we are satisfied, then we won't receive the meat of the Word that produces growth. Secondly, if we are satisfied, then we won't respond to opportunities to impact others. Other than the complete personal assurance of salvation, knowing that we have led others to that same saving knowledge of the Lord Jesus Christ may be one of the greatest opportunities of our lives.

THE NEW COVENANT PLAN

When we accept Jesus Christ as our Savior and Lord and our sins have been covered by His blood, the Holy Ghost baptizes us in the body of Christ. *"For by one Spirit are we all baptized into one body, whether we be Jews or Gentiles, whether we be bond or free, and have been all made to drink into one Spirit"* (1 Corinthians 12:13).

Then, the disciple baptizes us in water. Baptism in water is commanded by God for every believer. It is so important that even Jesus Himself was baptized in water. In Matthew 3:13, we see Jesus coming to His cousin, John, to be baptized. Jesus said that His water baptism was done in order to *"fulfill all righteousness."* He then went on to establish baptism as an eternal ordinance for His church, calling every believer to follow His pattern: *"Go therefore, and teach all nations, baptizing them in the name of the Father, and of the Son, and of the Holy Ghost"* (Matthew 28:19). Yes, it is symbolic, but the symbolism is a very powerful thing. A wedding ring is the outward symbol that you are married. A military uniform is the outward symbol that you proudly serve in the armed services of this country. Water baptism is the outward symbol designed by God to identify a person as a disciple of Jesus Christ. Water baptism is a wonderful funeral. It is an act of faith in which we testify both to God and to the world that the person we were before is dead and buried, and we are raised as a new creation in Christ. *"Therefore we are buried with Him by baptism into death: that like as Christ was raised up from the dead by the glory of the Father, even so we also should walk in newness of life"* (Romans 6:4). And, *"Buried with Him in baptism, wherein also you are risen with Him through the faith of the operation of God, Who raised Him (Jesus) from the dead"* (Colossians 2:12).

You have never read of an un-baptized Christian anywhere in the Bible. In fact, baptism immediately followed a person's salvation. When the people responded to Peter's sermon on the Day of Pentecost, Acts 2:38 says that he gave them the New Covenant plan: *"Repent, and be baptized every one of you in the name of Jesus Christ for the remission of sins, and you shall receive the gift of the Holy Ghost."* Verse 41 says they *"gladly received His word, and were baptized."* In Acts chapter 8, the apostle Phillip met a eunuch at Ethiopia and *"preached Jesus"* and the New Covenant plan to him, and the eunuch believed. He was so excited and ready, that as they *"went down the road, they came to some water. And the eunuch said, 'See, here is water. What hinders me from being baptized?' Then Phillip said, 'If you believe with all your heart, you may.' And he answered and said, 'I believe that Jesus Christ is the Son of God.' So he commanded the chariot to stand still. And both Philip and the eunuch went down into the water, and he baptized him* (Acts 8:36-38).

Being baptized is a command from God that is required of every believer. Jesus' last words according to Mark 16:16 says, *"He that believes and is baptized shall be saved, but he who does not believe shall be damned (condemned)."* When we receive God's saving grace, it is no accident that He calls us to identify with Him in a way that makes it real to us. If you are struggling with your past, it might be because you did not give the old you a proper burial! Water baptism is a wonderful reminder of God's saving grace. The person we were before is dead, and we are raised with Jesus as a totally new creation. *"Therefore if any man be in Christ, he is a new creature (creation); old things are passed away; behold all things are become new"* (2 Corinthians 5:17).

So, the Holy Ghost baptizes us into the body of Christ, the disciple baptizes us in water, and then, Jesus baptizes us with the Holy Ghost. This is the New Covenant plan! John the Baptist preached the gospel of repentance, and he also prophesied the baptism of the Spirit. *"I indeed baptize you with water unto repentance: but he that cometh after me is mightier than I, whose shoes I am not worthy to bear: he shall baptize you with the Holy Ghost, and with fire"* (Matthew 3:11, KJV).

This is very clearly different than what the Holy Spirit does to baptize us in the body of Christ. Grammatically, it is not the same. Theologically, it is not the same. It is not taught as the same by John the Baptist, by Jesus, by Peter, by Phillip, or by Paul. In every gospel of the New Testament (Matthew 3, Luke 3, Mark 1, and John 1), you will find the death, burial, and resurrection of Jesus, and you will find the Baptism with the Holy Spirit. John 1:32 portrays a beautiful picture of the New Covenant plan: *"And John bore witness, saying, 'I saw the Spirit descending from heaven like a dove, and He remained upon Him. I did not know Him, but He who sent me to baptize with water said to me, 'Upon whom you see the Spirit descending, and remaining on Him, this is He who baptizes with the Holy Spirit.' And I have seen and testified that this is the Son of God'"* (John 1:32-34).

In the Old Testament, the Spirit of God came upon people but never remained. In the New Testament (Covenant), God prepares His New Covenant plan with specific information about Jesus to John as He launched his ministry: *"And I knew him not: but he that sent me to baptize with water, the same said unto me, Upon whom thou shalt see the Spirit descending, and remaining on him, the same is he which baptizeth with the Holy Ghost"* (John 1:33, KJV). Which leads me to a simple question: If Jesus needed the Holy Ghost while here on earth, do we need to be baptized with the Holy Ghost? Yes! Next question: What is the New Covenant plan? Answer: Salvation (baptized in the body of Christ), Water (baptizing the old man and symbolic resurrection of the new man), and Spirit (baptism with the Holy Ghost). Acts 1:4 gives us the very last words of Christ on the earth: *"And being assembled together with them, He commanded them not to depart from Jerusalem, but to wait for the Promise of the Father, 'which,' He said, 'you have heard from Me; for John truly baptized with water, but you shall be baptized with the Holy Ghost not many days from now.'"* What was the promise? Jesus gave the promise (which had already been foretold by John the Baptist), *"And I will pray the Father, and He shall give you another Comforter, that He may abide with you forever. Even the Spirit of truth, Whom the world cannot receive, because it sees Him not, neither knows Him, but you know Him, for He dwells with you, and shall be in you. I will not leave you comfortless"* (John 14:16-18).

THE BAPTISM IN THE HOLY GHOST

Following Jesus' ascension, on the Day of Pentecost, 120 believers were filled with the Holy Ghost as was prophesied by the prophet Joel: *"And it shall come to pass afterward that I will pour out My Spirit on all flesh; Your sons and your daughters shall prophesy, your old men shall dream dreams, your young men shall see visions"* (Joel 2:28). While great crowds came running from far and near in awe and amazement as the Holy Ghost turned their city into a great evangelistic arena, Peter stood up to preach Jesus to the people. They were interested and eager to hear what he had to say as they had seen and heard something out of these 120 believers that they have never seen or heard before. It was under the anointing of the Holy Ghost that Peter preached Jesus, and the people heard and believed. They were *"pricked in their hearts, and said to Peter and the rest of the apostles, 'Men and brethren, what shall we do?' Then Peter said to them, 'Repent, and let every one of you be baptized in the name of Jesus Christ for the remission of sins, and you shall receive the gift of the Holy Ghost"* (Acts 2:37-38). So here is a question. Was the gift of the Holy Ghost just for the 120 Upper Room believers? That answer is found in verse 39: *"For the promise is to you and to your children, and to all who are afar off, as many as the Lord our God will call.'"*

Going further in the books of Acts, we find Philip continuing in this great work. *"But when they believed Philip preaching the things concerning the Kingdom of God, and the name of Jesus Christ, they were baptized, both men and women." "Now when the apostles who were at Jerusalem heard that Samaria had received the word of God, they sent Peter and John to them, who, when they had come down, prayed for them that they might receive the Holy Spirit. For as yet He had fallen upon none of them. They had only been baptized in the name of the Lord Jesus. Then they laid hands on them, and they received the Holy Spirit"* (Acts 8:12, 14-17). Question: Why would the disciples go pray for people to receive the Holy Ghost if they had already been filled with the Holy Ghost?

Consider this question and similar Biblical answers in the following Scriptures:

> "*Ananias went his way, and entered into the house and putting his hands on him said, 'Brother Saul, the Lord Jesus that appeared unto you in the way as you came, has sent me, that you might receive your sight, and be filled with the Holy Ghost* (Acts 9:17).

> "*While Peter yet spoke these words, the Holy Ghost fell on all of them which heard the word, and they of the circumcision* (the Jews) *which believed were astonished, as many as came with Peter, because that on the Gentiles also was poured out the gift of the Holy Ghost. For they heard them speak with tongues, and magnify God* (Acts 10:44-46).

As Paul passed through Ephesus, he found disciples of John and "*he said unto them, 'Have ye received the Holy Ghost since ye believed?' And they said unto him, 'We have not so much as heard whether there be any Holy Ghost.' And he said unto them, 'Unto what then were ye baptized?' And they said, 'Unto John's baptism.' Then said Paul, 'John verily baptized with the baptism of repentance, saying unto the people, that they should believe on him which should come after him, that is, on Christ Jesus.' When they heard this, they were baptized in the name of the Lord Jesus. And when Paul had laid his hands upon them, the Holy Ghost came on them; and they spake with tongues, and prophesied*" (Acts 19:2-6, KJV).

One more time, let's review the New Covenant plan: the Holy Ghost baptizes us into the body of Christ, the disciple baptizes us in water, and then, Jesus baptizes us with the Holy Ghost.

WHY TONGUES?

Now, let's answer one other oft-asked question regarding the baptism with the Holy Ghost: Why speak in other tongues?

First, speaking in tongues is speaking in a language. According to Acts 2:6, many people traveling from abroad heard the gospel of Jesus Christ in their language. This is a miracle! Having said that, the first thing that the Holy Spirit changes is the tongue. Why? Because the one thing we have the most difficulty in controlling is the tongue. *"The tongue is a little member, and boasts great things.... And the tongue is a fire, a world of iniquity; so is the tongue among our members, that it defiles the whole body, and sets on fire the course of nature, and it is set on fire of hell"* (James 3:5-6). The NIV translation says, *"The tongue also is a fire, a world of evil among the parts of the body. It corrupts the whole body, sets the whole course of one's life on fire, and is itself set on fire by hell."*

These new believers had to submit or yield to the Holy Ghost. Babies do not speak fluently, and many believers just filled with the Spirit may not speak "fluently." And, that's okay. When you are baptized in the Holy Ghost, you should not be concerned about the "how" of speaking in tongues. Regardless of your verbal proficiency, your Heavenly Father loves it!

Secondly, it is a language of the Spirit. *"For he that speaketh in an unknown tongue speaketh not unto men, but unto God: for no man understandeth him; howbeit in the spirit he speaketh mysteries"* (1 Corinthians 14:2, KJV). This is very clear — he who speaks in an unknown tongue speaks in the Spirit. What is spoken is a mystery to everyone except God. *"For if I pray in an unknown tongue, my spirit prayeth, but my understanding is unfruitful"* (v.14). Or, as the New Living Translation says, *"For if I pray in tongues, my spirit is praying, but I do not understand what I'm saying."* Simply meaning, I do not understand it in my mind. *"What is the conclusion then? I will pray with the spirit, and I will also pray with the understanding. I will sing with the spirit, and I will also sing with the understanding"* (v.15). This is very clear and this is what the Bible says. I pray every day in English — that is my understanding. I listen to other people pray in English — that is my understanding. But I also pray in the spirit. That is the mystery to me, but my spirit is talking directly to God.

Question: Why do that? Answer: Because the Bible says there are things about which you do not know how to pray. *"Likewise the Spirit also helps in our weaknesses. For we do not know what we should pray for as we ought, but the Spirit Himself makes intercession for us with groanings which cannot be uttered. Now, He who searches the hearts knows what the mind of the Spirit is, because He makes intercession for the saints according to the will of God. And we know that all things work together for good to those who love God ..."* (Romans 8:26-28).

Is it possible that the Spirit has more understanding than I have about my situation? I am a person made up of three parts — spirit, soul, and body. My soul is my mind, will, and emotion. Many people only pray with their mind — what they understand. Are there any areas in my life that I do not understand? Yes! How do I pray effectively about something that I do not understand? Paul, the greatest New Testament apostle that ever lived, stressed three times in 1 Corinthians 14 the significance of praying in tongues. Verse 5 — *"I would that you all speak with tongues."* Verse 18 — *"I thank my God, I speak in tongues more than you all."* And, in verse 39 — *"... forbid not to speak with tongues."* How can someone say they do not believe in something that Paul explicitly said do not forbid anyone from doing it? How can anyone say that any gift of the Holy Ghost is of the devil? How can anyone say that any gift of the Spirit is not for today?

Perhaps the truth about this controversy is found in Proverbs 18:21 — *"Death and life are in the power of the tongue...."* Perhaps this is God's perfect way to submit your tongue to His Spirit, and the Holy Spirit can control your tongue! Praying in tongues is part of your spiritual armor found in Ephesians 6, with the final piece of the armor being *"praying always with all prayer and supplication in the Spirit"* (v.18). This goes perfectly with Jude 20: *"But you, beloved, building yourselves up on your most holy faith, praying in the Spirit."* I need the whole armor of God to be the most effective in all my spiritual battles. I need to be built up to my highest level of faith and power and to be the most effective in all my spiritual battles. I need to pray in the Spirit, and not just in my own understanding, to be the most effective in all my spiritual battles.

Third, speaking in other tongues is a pure language. This leads us to Genesis 11:1 — *"And the whole earth was of one language, and of one speech."* What language was that? Is it possible it was God's heavenly language? Before the Tower of Babel, languages (plural) had not yet been created. There was one language, from the time of Adam and Eve in the garden, for they walked and talked with God. We see God's emphasis on the power of language, for *"the Lord came down to see the city and the tower which the sons of men had built. And the Lord said, 'Indeed the people are one and they all have one language, and this is what they begin to do; now nothing that they propose to do will be withheld from them. Come, let Us go down and there confuse their language, that they may not understand one another's speech"* (Genesis 11:5-7). When the Lord created languages, they were scattered throughout the land, and the project at Babel was stopped.

God said, "They have one language and they can do anything that they come to an agreement to do." In other words, "All things are possible." Is it possible, that when you pray in the Spirit, that you come into the fullness of the revelation of all things being possible? Why? Because you are not praying soul-ish (mind) prayers, you are praying spiritual prayers. Let's face it, sometimes our prayers are selfish prayers — go back to James 4:3 from the New Living Translation — *"And even when you ask, you do not get it because your motives are all wrong — you want only what will give you pleasure."*

We know all about the prophecy concerning the Holy Ghost from Joel 2, but let me show you an even better reference in Zephaniah 3:9 — *"For then I will restore to the peoples a pure language, that they all may call on the name of the Lord, to serve Him with one accord."* Notice the word "restore" — God is saying I confused the languages in Genesis because the people at Babel were self-willed, not Spirit-willed. And now that the people are being filled with my Spirit, here is the sign — they will all have one pure language again. Where else do we see those two words, "one accord?" Acts 2:1! *"When the Day of Pentecost had fully come, they were all with one accord in one place."*

UNKNOWN TONGUES AND OTHER TONGUES

Now, let's move one step farther: *"For he who speaks in an unknown tongue does not speak to men but to God, for no one understands him; however, in the Spirit he speaks mysteries. But he that prophesies speaks unto men to edification, and exhortation, and comfort. He that speaks in an unknown tongue edifies himself, but he that prophesies edifies the church"* (1 Corinthians 14:2-4). Tongues operate in two levels, as confirmed very clearly in 1 Corinthians 14. Very simply, we have *unknown* tongues and *other* tongues. When the Spirit speaks through you, this is other tongues, which can be interpreted. This is one type of prophesying — it is the Holy Ghost speaking through you to the church. It is important for other tongues to be interpreted because we want to know what the Spirit is saying. Seven times in the book of Revelation, Jesus says, *"He that has an ear, let him hear what the Spirit says unto the churches."* The Spirit is speaking through you, but it is for us and we want to know what He is saying. Paul is very practical about this; he understood the necessity for the body of Christ to be edified. He understood the importance of order and excellence. *"How is it, brethren? When you come together, every one of you has a psalm, has a doctrine, has a tongue, has a revelation, has an interpretation. Let all things be done unto edification. If any man speak in tongues, let it be by two, or at the most by three, and that by course, and let one interpret. But if there be no interpreter, let him keep silence in the church, and let speak to himself, and to God. For you may all prophesy one by one, that all may learn, and all may be comforted. And the spirits of the prophets are subject to the prophets. For God is not the author of confusion, but of peace, as in all church of the saints. Wherefore, brethren, covet to prophesy, and forbid not to speak with tongues. Let all things be done decently and in order"* (1 Corinthians 14:26-28, 31-33, 39-40).

This is different from *"he that prays in an unknown tongue"* (verse 2), as this is not for interpretation — *"he speaks not unto men, but unto God; for no man understands him, howbeit in the Spirit he speaks mysteries."* This is not God speaking to us, this is us speaking to God. Even in the presence of the gift of interpretation, there is nothing to interpret. It is a mystery to everyone but God. In other words, it is none of your business. When I pray in an unknown tongue, He keeps me out of my business. Praying in the Spirit is for those times that either you cannot trust your mind or you simply do not know. *"The Spirit also helps our infirmities, for we know not what we should pray for as we ought; but the Spirit himself makes intercession for us with groanings which cannot be uttered. And he that searches the hearts knows what is the mind of the Spirit, because He makes intercession for the saints according to the will of God"* (Romans 8:26-27).

One of the greatest things we can do is think less and listen more when we pray. Our finite minds cannot understand the infinite plans of God, and even if God revealed everything to us, we still would not understand it all. God hides His plans for our future from our minds, but He reveals our future in our spirit. When you pray in an unknown tongue, you are absolutely praying the perfect and divine will of God for your life! There are some things in your life that you just do not know what to do and you do not know how to pray. You do not know whether to pray, "God, bring me out of it" or "God, bring it out of me."

Sometimes we just do not know what the will of God is in specific life circumstances. You may not know God's will about the guy you are thinking about marrying. You love him and he says he loves you, but you really want to know God's will. You cannot pray what is in your mind because that guy has already got your mind! This is why you must be able to pray in the Spirit. When you pray in the Spirit you are praying according to God's desires revealed by the Spirit. It goes beyond what we naturally see and hear, and allows our spiritual eyes and ears to have revelation of God's perfect will and plan. *"Eye has not seen, nor ear heard, neither have entered into the heart of man, the things which God has prepared for them that love Him; But God has revealed them unto us by His Spirit; for the Spirit searches all things, yea, the deep things of God"* (1 Corinthians 2:9-10).

CHAPTER 7

EMBRACE THE GOOD STUFF

"Prove all things; hold fast that which is good." Why are there so many different opinions on what the Bible says? Why are there so many different denominations, organizations, and fellowships in the church world? Who is right about what?

The rise of denominations within the Christian faith can be traced back to the Protestant Reformation, the movement to "reform" the Roman Catholic Church during the 16th century, out of which four major divisions or traditions of Protestantism would emerge: Lutheran, Reformed, Anabaptist, and Anglican. From these four, other denominations grew over the centuries.

The Lutheran denomination was named after Martin Luther and was based on his teachings. The Methodists got their name because their founder, John Wesley, was famous for teaching "methods" for spiritual growth. Presbyterians are named for their views of church leadership — the Greek word for elder is "presbyteros." Baptists got their name because they emphasized the importance of baptism.

I was "born and raised" Pentecostal, and Tresa and I are ordained ministers with the Pentecostal Church of God. Obviously, this book is written from a Pentecostal perspective. My parents have been members of the same independent Pentecostal church my entire life. In the past 30 years of ministry, I have preached for congregations labeled as independent

Pentecostal, Pentecostal Holiness, Church of God, Assembly of God, Church of God in Christ, Hebrew Pentecostal, Charismatic, non-denominational, and inter-denominational — all under the Pentecostal "label." All the same, yet unique. Our overall distinctiveness primarily stems from Acts 2, when 120 believers in an upper room were baptized in the Holy Ghost and spoke with other tongues. Typically, our basic doctrinal standards are consistent with other evangelical Protestants, regarding the inerrancy of Scripture, salvation by grace through faith in the Lord Jesus Christ, the second coming of Christ, and Heaven and Hell.

Most believe that the origin of modern Pentecostalism can be traced to Bethel Bible College in Topeka, Kansas. Founded by Charles Parham in 1900, he and his students believed that the Scriptures give indisputable proof that speaking with other tongues is the initial physical evidence of the baptism with the Holy Ghost. On January 1, 1901 the first day of the 20th century, Agnes Ozman requested those present to lay hands on her and pray that she might receive the infilling with the Holy Ghost. When this was done she began to speak in tongues, glorifying God. It was reported that she was so overwhelmed by this new experience of Pentecostal power she could not speak in the English language for three days. Miss Ozman's baptism inspired the other students to seek for a similar experience. After three days of continual prayer, many others, including Parham, received the mighty infilling of the Spirit.

Afterwards, Parham carried this Pentecostal message across the heartland of America. William J. Seymour, an African-American holiness preacher from Louisiana, heard Parham's teaching in Houston, and carried it to Los Angeles. Ultimately, a former African Methodist Episcopal (AME) building at 312 Azusa Street became the location for a continuous three-year revival that has known around the world.

Until the 1920's, with the exception of the Holiness-Pentecostal churches in the southeast, there was little formal organization. Independent Pentecostal churches were formed in any available setting where eager believers could assemble. Since the congregations tended to trust anyone claiming to be Spirit-filled, they were often taken advantage of by shysters. Therefore, it became apparent that some form of fellowship was necessary to protect the message and integrity of the Pentecostal revival.[5]

The organizational histories of the Pentecostal Church of God, the Assembly of God, the Church of God in Christ, and many other great Pentecostal denominations are well-documented, and need not to be repeated. Likewise, are the histories and doctrines of the Baptists, the Methodists, or any of the other 6000+ organized Protestant denominations. More importantly, while many of these organizations have different doctrinal views and methods of worship, they are united in this central, essential foundation: Jesus Christ is the one and only Lord and Savior.

Perhaps this was Paul's concern as we observe the early development of the New Testament Church. Paul was very plain in his admonition that Christ must remain the central theme of the church: "Now I say this, that each of you says, 'I am of Paul,' or 'I am of Apollos,' or 'I am of Cephas,' or 'I am of Christ.' Is Christ divided? Was Paul crucified for you? Or were you baptized in the name of Paul" (1 Corinthians 1:12-13)? And to reiterate and emphasize his point, there is little confusion in this question: "For when one says, 'I am of Paul,' and another 'I am of Apollos,' are you not carnal (1 Corinthians 3:4)?

Our differences and divisions stem from sincere, albeit flawed, believers committed to upholding the foundations of our Biblical beliefs as we understand them with a clear conscience and pure motives. With the words "differences" and "divisions" in this statement, should we ignore or denounce denominations? I think not. As believers, should we just not go to church and worship on our own at home? No! We should seek out a body of believers where the Gospel of Christ is preached, where each member is encouraged to have a personal relationship with the Lord, and where Biblical ministry opportunities are provided to spread the gospel and glorify God. The church is important and we need relationships that can only be found in the body of believers, with positive Godly support and a faith community in which to serve. We should seek out a church where the pastor is preaching the Gospel without fear or favor and is encouraged to do so. As believers, there are certain basic doctrines that we must believe, but beyond that, there is latitude on how we can serve and worship. It is this latitude where the positives of denominations, organizations, and fellowships outweigh the negatives. Diversity allows us to be individuals in Christ; disunity divides and destroys. Diversity is a powerful force whereby we can unite in our gifts and abilities to build the Kingdom of Christ on earth. In spite of our labels, or our varied interpretation of some Scriptures, there is only one church — one body of believers — and our goal is to preserve and protect the beautiful bride of Christ as caretakers of that which is precious in the eyes of our Groom.

THE WHOLE COUNSEL OF GOD

It is inherent in each individual to embrace a set of beliefs. When it comes to our spiritual beliefs, it is important to resist selectivism — using the Scripture to prove one is right, while ignoring or twisting the Scriptures that prove them wrong. Peter warns against the danger of "wresting" — twisting and turning the Scriptures — which is actually symptomatic of ignorance and instability (2 Peter 3:16, KJV). Paul encouraged the believers to embrace unity, resist immaturity, and reject using the Bible for personal gain: *"… till we all come to the unity of the faith and of the knowledge of the Son of God, to a perfect man, to the measure of the stature of the fullness of Christ; that we should no longer be children, tossed to and fro and carried about with every wind of doctrine, by the trickery of men, in the cunning craftiness of deceitful plotting, but, speaking the truth in love …."* (Ephesians 4:13-15).

When we receive and embrace the Word in its entirety, the Holy Ghost is not limited in His ability to bring revelation to us. The teaching and preaching of the Word is received with gladness and our differences highlight the beauty of our individual gifts, not opportunities to divide. Any group is made stronger when diversity is embraced. Paul encouraged the believers to value the power of spiritual revelation, as first spoken by Isaiah (64:4): *"But as it is written: "Eye has not seen, nor ear heard, nor have entered into the heart of man the things which God has prepared for those who love Him. But God has revealed them to us through His Spirit. For the Spirit searches all things, yes, the deep things of God."* The Holy Ghost reveals things to you that you cannot understand any other way. You can read the Bible your whole life, but it is only when the Holy Ghost speaks to you that He reveals His Spirit to you. You can say you are a Christian all you want (and a lot of people do), but it is only when I allow the Holy Ghost to give me revelation of the lordship of the Lord Jesus Christ in my life that then, and only then, by the Spirit that I learn submission to His lordship, and then, and only then, I can say that Jesus is Lord (1 Corinthians 12:3).

You are the sum total of what you listen to, who you hang with, who you run with, who you talk on the phone with, who you interact with, and who you run to when you are in trouble. If someone has your ear, then they have influence (counsel) in your life. Question: How much time do I spend listening to the Holy Ghost? If He has my ear, then He influences me. If I call my mom every time I have trouble, my mom is my influence. If I call Sally May every time I need to talk to someone, than Sally May is my influence. All of us do need someone, and dear friends and godly people of wisdom are invaluable. My great concern is that we are often drawn to people of trouble, not success. How can I be encouraged and enlightened if the people I call may have more problems than me? There may be marginal marital advice from a friend who has been divorced numerous times. There may be marginal parenting advice from a friend who did not even raise his own children. There is no good financial advice to be gained from broke folks. They can't help you. Get around people who are successful in doing things that you want to do. Otherwise, you are not looking for help, you are looking for company (yes, misery loves company). Reject chaos, confusion, and clutter *"for God is not the author of confusion but of peace, as in all the churches of the saints"* (1 Corinthians 14:33).

Slow down and hear what God is saying to your life. There are people that we all know whose lives are going "a hundred miles an hour," but never get anything done. Why? It is a tool of distraction used by our enemy; it is a blinding technique. Consider three powerful, peaceful Scriptures:

"Be still, and know that I am God..." (Psalm 46:10).

"In returning and rest you shall be saved; in quietness and confidence shall be your strength" (Isaiah 30:15).

"... Aspire to lead a quiet life, to mind your own business, and to work with your own hands...." (1 Thessalonians 4:11).

Say this plainly and say it often: "I will learn to keep my big mouth shut and mind my own business!" If I am busily focused on you, I cannot hear what the Holy Ghost is saying to me. Did you ever allow yourself to get wrapped up in someone else's mess, trying to solve their problems, ready to fight their enemies ... and it is not even your problem? Why would you get mad and un-sanctified over someone else's problems? Refuse to give that kind of control of your life to another person. We do not need to be distracted by drama. We must have the ability speak clearly to the Father, and hear what the Father is saying to us.

HEARING WHAT GOD SEES

After the miracle of fire on Mount Carmel, the prophet Elijah, accompanied only by one servant, went up higher on the mountain to a quiet place. The miracle of fire falling from the heavens was amazing; the unified response of the confused people was the equivalent of a one-day national revival. But, the work was not yet completed. *"Elijah went up to the top of Carmel; then he bowed down on the ground, and put his face between his knees"* (1 Kings 18:42).

Why did he put his face between his knees? Perhaps this was his moment of saying, "I do not want to see anyone, nor hear from anyone. Right now, I need to hear from the Lord." It is liberating when we can graciously say to those around us who are consumed in their drama, "I love you, but I will not enable you." "I love you, but not your foolishness." "I love you, but the primary voice in my life is the Holy Ghost." Why is this important? It keeps our "Eyes Wide Open!"

There is no time to be distracted or manipulated. Manipulators come in all sizes and varieties. Your two-year -old can be a manipulator. Your best friend can be a manipulator. Co-workers can be manipulators. Satan is the master manipulator in the earth. Adam and Eve walked with God in the Garden of Eden, yet the master manipulator was successful in changing the course of mankind forever. How? Satan appeals to their senses. God works in the spiritual, Satan works in the sensual. Feelings are natural, but feelings can be deceptive. The mind is powerful, but the godly are led by the Spirit, not by their feelings.

Faith does not always make sense. It did not make sense to march around the walls of Jericho. It did not make sense to give the man of God your last piece of bread when you and your child are one meal away from death by starvation. It did not make sense to offer a basket lunch to 5000 hungry people. It did not make sense to step out of a boat in the middle of a hurricane. Faith requires the fullness of spiritual revelation, not feelings and emotions.

Sensual people will disappear in your life as your spirit man develops because they do not understand where you are. To sensual people, it does not make sense to go to church every Sunday, it does not make sense to tithe, it does not make sense to pray. God does not make sense and faith does not make sense. God is not sensual, God is spiritual. *"God is Spirit, and those who worship Him must worship in spirit and truth"* (John 4:24).

Here is a statement that will bring ridicule from many: "I listen to what He tells me to do and I do it." This is not flaky nor some form of mental instability — this is spiritual maturity. Spiritual maturity is believing and receiving the fullness of God's Word, developing in spiritual knowledge, and joining in unity under the leadership and guidance of godly men and women who care for our souls, in the great and glorious body of Christ — the church, the Bride of Christ.

We are His bride, Christ is the groom. The great marriage ceremony is in the last moments of preparation. The exact date remains unknown, but we have been given much information by His Word, His prophets, and by Divine revelation to know that our time is soon. Every day is one day closer, and the importance of living each day as if it is our last cannot be overstated. And until He appears, we will keep our "Eyes Wide Open."

CHAPTER 8

THE GRACE COVERED LIFE

In our 21st Century society, discontentment and stress along with emotional, mental and marital discord may be at an all-time high. Likewise, believers are dealing with attacks against their lives, and this is happening in the midst of what appears to be the greatest hour of the church. We have the greatest praise and worship that we have ever had. We have great singers, bands, dancers, preachers, teachers, and great expositors of the Word. Bibles are readily available. Christian television and radio are available 24 hours a day. We have access to preaching and teaching on the internet, easily attainable on your computer, your iPad, and your cell phone, anytime and anywhere. It is estimated that there are more than 300,000 Protestant churches in America. [6] Most people have a car, and the ones that do not are provided transportation to a local church by bus and van ministries. Often, there is usually a church within walking distance of many homes in any given city. How is it that at what should be our finest moment, we see the greatest attack? The answer to that is simple: we are living in the last days. The devil knows he has a short time to work, and he is throwing everything he has at every believer. (*See* Revelation 12:12.)

Now, that is an answer, but it is not the full answer. If we are walking in the power of Christ that belongs to the end-time glorious church, why do some of our dearest friends fail in spiritual attacks? That is a much deeper question that requires us to look at ourselves with "Eyes Wide Open." Why is church attendance at the lowest it has ever been in the history of our nation when there is the most availability to it? A summary of a recent Barna Group survey says this: "American Christians are not as devoted to their faith as they would like to believe. They have positive feelings about the importance of their faith, but their faith is rarely the focal point of their life, nor is it a critical factor in their decision making. They have very limited time or effort devoted to spiritual growth. People are trying to discover how to fit God into their increasingly fragmented, busy and changing lives — they just are not sure how to pencil God into their schedules. When comparing the lifestyle choices of born-again Christians to the national norms, there are more areas of similarity than distinction." [7]

Whatever you feed will flourish. People who constantly rehearse their problems — what is going wrong and what is wrong with their marriage, their home, their job, and their church — find that their problems always get worse. Whatever you focus on is what grows in your life. Thankfully, that goes both ways. If I focus on the good, the good grows. Marriages that get a lot of attention from the partners should get stronger. Parents who spend quality time with their kids should have good relationships with their kids. If you love your church, you will be excited about its growth and what you receive from every service. If you spend time in the Word every day, you will keep growing in your relationship with God. Whatever you feed will grow.

TRANSFORMATION

As I discussed in detail earlier, we are complex beings made up of three parts — body, soul (mind), and spirit. When you are born again, your spirit man is changed by the Spirit of God. The soul (the mind) is what we work on every day — *"be not conformed to this world, but be transformed by the renewing of your mind"* (Romans 12:2). Your body has lusts, but who it obeys is solely dependent on who is in charge. You are not an animal, so you do not just do what you do out of instinct. You do what you do based on who is in charge of your life, and there will always be a conflict here. Paul said in Romans 7:18, *"For I know that in me (that is, in my flesh) nothing good dwells. For to will is present with me, but how to perform what is good I do not find. For the good that I will do, I do not do; but the evil I will not to do, that I practice. Not if I do what I will not to do, it is no longer I who do it, but sin that dwells in me. I find then a law, that evil is present with me, the one who wills to do good. For I delight in the law of God according to the inward man."*

Sounds like we are condemned to a lifetime of guilt and conflict, doesn't it? Not true! Look at Romans chapter 8, beginning with verse 1: *"There is therefore now no condemnation to those who are in Christ Jesus, who do walk according to the flesh, but according to the Spirit. For the law of the Spirit of life in Christ Jesus has made me free from the law of sin and death."* Verse 5: *"For those who live according to the flesh set their minds on the things of the flesh, but those who live according to the Spirit, the things of the Spirit. For to be carnally minded is death, but to be spiritually minded is life and death."* Verse 8: *"So then, those who are in the flesh cannot please God. But you are not in the flesh but in the Spirit, if indeed the Spirit of God dwells in you."*

Here is where the hyper-grace movement followers may disagree with me. They would say, "Well, if you are saved, there is no condemnation because we're under grace. No matter what you do, it does not change your relationship with God. At the moment of faith and confession of Jesus Christ as Savior, we are automatically and eternally forgiven without reservation. Do your best, grace will cover the rest." However, Romans 6:1 asks a powerful question: *"What shall we say then? Shall we continue in sin that grace may abound? God forbid! How shall we that are dead to sin live any longer therein? Know ye not, that as many of us were baptized into Jesus Christ were baptized into His death? Therefore, we are buried with Him by baptism into death: that like as Christ was raised up from the dead by the glory of the Father, even so we also should walk in newness of life."* Verse 14: *"Sin does not have dominion over you* (condemnation)*: for you are not under the law, but under grace."*

The condemnation is not the preacher making you feel bad because your particular pet sin was dealt with in last Sunday's sermon. The concept of condemnation is talking about the fact that I have not been condemned to a lifetime of the struggle. Yes, we are tempted; yes, we will fail; and yes, we are all a work in progress. But I have good gospel news — grace is at work in the **transformation** process, not the cover-up process!

> *"For the grace of God that brings salvation has appeared to all men, teaching us that, denying ungodliness and worldly lusts, we should live soberly, righteously, and godly in the present world, looking for the blessed hope and glorious appearing of our great God and Savior Jesus Christ, Who gave Himself for us, that He might redeem us from every lawless deed and purify for Himself His own special people, zealous for good works"* (Titus 2:11-14).

> *"Who is the man that desires life, and loves many days that he may see good? Keep your tongue from evil, and your lips from speaking deceit. Depart from evil and do good. Seek peace and pursue it. The eyes of the Lord are over the righteous, and His ears are open to their cry. The face of the Lord is against them that do evil, to cut off the remembrance of them from the earth. The righteous cry out, and the Lord hears, and delivers them out of all their troubles"* (Psalm 34:12-17).

> *"Moreover, brethren, I do not want you to be unaware that all our fathers were under the cloud, all passed through the sea, all were baptized into Moses in the cloud and the sea, all ate the same spiritual food, and all drank the same spiritual drink. For they drank of that spiritual Rock that followed them, and that Rock was Christ. But with most of them God was not well pleased, for their bodies were scattered in the wilderness. Now these things became our examples, to the intent that we should not lust after evil things as they also lusted. And do not become idolaters as were some of them. As it is written,*

'The people sat down to eat and drink, and rose up to play.' Nor let us commit sexual immorality, as some of them did, and in one day 23,000 fell (Israelite men had open sexual relationships with the Moabite women — see Numbers 25); *nor let us tempt Christ, as some of them also tempted, and were destroyed of serpents* (the people complained about their journey, and said they "loathed" the manna God gave them — see Numbers 21); *nor complain, as some of them also complained, and were destroyed by the destroyer* (Hebrews 3 says that all died in the wilderness because of their doubt and unbelief). *Now all these things happened to them as examples, and they were written for our admonition, upon whom the ends of the ages have come. Therefore let him who thinks he stands take heed lest he fall. No temptation has overtaken you except such as is common to man; but God is faithful, who will not allow you to be tempted beyond what you are able, but with the temptation will also make the way of escape, that you may be able to bear it"* (1 Corinthians 10:1-13).

"Be diligent to present yourself approved before God, a worker who does not need to be ashamed, rightly dividing the word of truth. But shun profane and idle babblings, for they will increase to more ungodliness." Verse 19: *"Nevertheless the solid foundation of God stands, having this seal: 'The Lord knows those who are His,' and, 'Let everyone who names the name of Christ depart from iniquity.'"* Verse 21: *"Flee youthful lusts, but pursue righteousness, faith, love, peace with those who call on the Lord out of a pure heart. But avoid foolish and ignorant disputes, knowing that they generate strife. And a servant of the Lord must not quarrel but be gentle to all, able to teach, patient, in humility correcting those who are in opposition, if God perhaps will grant them repentance, so that they may know the truth, and that they may come to their senses and escape the snare of the devil, having been taken captive by him to do his will"* (2 Timothy 2:15-26).

THE COVENANTS

The shift from clear biblical preaching and doctrinal teaching to a speaker-led motivational seminar in the modern church is readily apparent. The refusal or reluctance to mention the need for repentance, or to teach on topics like hell and judgment is glaring. And, while the 21st-century church may see this trend as more prevalent, this is nothing new. For centuries the body of Christ has wrestled with something called *antinomianism* ("against the law") — the moral law of the Old Testament has been done away with and once we are in Christ, there is free grace in which we can live as we choose since we are not under the Law but under grace. Thus, according to this view, the Old Testament is not that important to read except for metaphors, types and shadows, and symbols regarding the coming of Christ. The New Testament is all about grace and does away with the Old Testament Law. I concede this may be my over-simplified view, but I believe the concept of the intent is correct.

Under the grace covenant, the teaching of the Ten Commandments was taught throughout the New Testament writings. *"Children, obey your parents in the Lord, for this is right. 'Honor your father and mother,' which is the first commandment with promise; 'that it may be well with you and you may live long on the earth'"* (Ephesians 6:1-3). *"You shall not covet"* is quoted in Romans 7:7, and *"Do not commit adultery"* and *"do not murder"* is quoted in James 2:11. Obedience to the Ten Commandments (the moral law) is also taught indirectly, as in 1 John 5:21, which instructs believers to stay away from idols (from the second commandment, regarding not making a carved image to worship). Jesus said that the greatest commandment in the Law is to love God with all the heart, mind and soul (see Matthew 22:37-38), which corresponds to the first commandment regarding having no other gods before Him.

Paul states three distinct principles towards the law under the grace covenant in the book of Romans. First, we dishonor God when we disobey the (moral) law. *"You who make your boast in the law, do you dishonor God through breaking the law"* (Romans 2:23)? Secondly, the law is holy, righteous and good. *"Therefore the law is holy, and the commandments holy and just and good"* (Romans 7:12). And, finally, the purpose of being filled with the Spirit of Christ is so the righteousness of the law would be fulfilled in us. *"For what the law could not do in that it was weak through the flesh, God did by sending His own Son in the likeness of sinful flesh, on account of sin; He condemned sin in the flesh, that the righteousness requirement of the law might be fulfilled in us who do not walk according to the flesh but according to the Spirit"* (Romans 8:3-4).

A grace-covered life has standards for obedience and disobedience. Although we cannot be saved by following the Law (because everyone is guilty of breaking the Law, according to Romans 3:19), God uses the moral law as the standard of righteousness in which to judge us of sin. Though the Law does not save us, the knowledge of it sanctifies us when we yield to the power of the Holy Spirit dwelling in us. *"Therefore by the deeds of the law no flesh will be justified in His sight, for by the law is the knowledge of sin"* (Romans 3:20). Yes, the next verse says *"the righteousness of God apart from the law is revealed"*, and verse 24 says we are *"justified freely by His grace through the redemption that is in Christ Jesus."* But we must not confuse the difference between ceremonial law and moral law. Ceremonial law such as circumcision and animal sacrifices were nullified in Christ Jesus, the perfect Lamb of God who took away the sins of the whole world. In Him, by a single offering of Himself, He abolished the law of commandments and record of debt that were against us. In Him, we are no longer obligated to follow the Levitical system, for the New Covenant clearly is a more perfect continuation of the Old Covenant because of its prophetic fulfillment in Jesus the Christ. *"For the law, having a shadow of the good things to come, and not the very image of the things, can never with these same sacrifices, which they offer continually year by year, make those who approach perfect."* Verse 5: *"Therefore, when He came into the world, He said, 'Sacrifice and offering You did not desire, but a body You have prepared for Me. In burnt offerings and sacrifices for sin You had no pleasure. Then I said, "Behold, I have come — in* the volume of the book it is written of Me — to do Your will, O God." Verse 10: "By that will we have been sanctified through the offering of the body of Jesus Christ once for all."

For the sake of exposing the dangers of "hyper-grace", I will continue to rightfully affirm holiness, yet without legalism. It is right to speak against sin, and not just in the context of forgiveness of sins in Christ. It is right to take a stand for righteousness, even in the face of ungoverned political correctness run amok. It is right to show the inseparable connection between the Old and New Testament — the New Covenant brought forth perfection, not eradication. It is right to hold our spiritual leaders accountable to godly living. It is right to embrace the biblically-based doctrines and conservative values that are the foundations of our great churches. I fear that the over-used and much-maligned term "old school" makes us appear irrelevant and causes many to dismiss the very principles of our faith that have made us impactful and relevant in a sin-filled world. A true prophetic voice and spiritual revelation come to holy and consecrated people, as this has been God's design from the beginning. *"For the prophecy came not in old time by the will of man; but **holy men of God** spake as they were moved by the Holy Ghost"* (2 Peter 1:21, KJV) [emphasis added].

AMAZING GRACE

Now, having said all that, I will be "fair and balanced" — not all ministers that may be considered "hyper-grace" condone sinful living. They state that God's true grace will produce a holy life, and I believe them when they say that and I certainly agree. As has been stated, "We are not propagating immorality because if we truly believe in God and love Him there will be corresponding works (because faith without works is dead)."[8] Well, I will say amen to that! Furthermore, it is important to note that legalism and narrow doctrinal dogma has brought about its own casualties. Many believers have found freedom and deliverance through the message of grace after living under a weight of condemnation and oppressive religion, trying to be accepted by a holy God if only they could just live a good enough life to be pleasing to the Lord.

Believers often struggle with guilty consciences, failing to realize the depth of God's love for them and failing to understand what Jesus did on their behalf. The revelation of grace is a perfect solution to combat guilt and shame. The teaching power of grace instructs us in holiness. Grace is glorious both in its liberty and in its instruction — you can never be more righteous than you are the moment that your sins are covered by the blood of Jesus Christ. You can develop in your walk with God in holiness and learn how to *"abstain from all appearance of evil"* (KJV). Paul's writing to Titus is genius in this revelation: *"For the grace of God that brings salvation has appeared to all men, teaching us that, denying ungodliness and worldly lusts, we should live soberly, righteously, and godly in the present age, looking for the blessed hope and glorious appearing of our great God and Savior Jesus Christ, who gave Himself for us, that He might redeem us from every lawless deed and purify for Himself His own special people, zealous for good works"* (Titus 2:11-14). And he was emphatic in his declaration to both those who received this glorious word, as well as those who resisted it! *"Speak these things, exhort, and rebuke with all authority"* (v.15).

CHOICES

The choices we make in life are directly correlated to the choices God has made for us. To many of us, it sometimes takes a while (or maybe even a long while) for us to discern what God has decided for us. When he said, "I refuse to be called the son of Pharaoh's daughter" (Hebrews 11:24), Moses did not know that God had chosen him to be the deliverer of millions enslaved in Egypt. In addition to that, God gave Moses the commandments and the law, what will forever be called the Mosaic Law. He did not know what God had decided for him based on the choice he made. God chose Moses, but He did not choose Moses' sons to take a place of leadership. God chose Joshua. Joshua was the one that went up with Moses and spent 40 days on the side of the holy mountain, not knowing exactly what Moses was doing, or what was happening between him and his God. He stayed there in faith and obedience and trust. And by so doing, God chose Joshua to succeed Moses.

Jonathan is a wonderful character study in the Bible. God did not choose Jonathan. Jonathan was the crown prince of Israel, but God chose David, a shepherd boy, as the next king. Even though he was the heir-apparent, he had the character and understanding to know that it was David who was anointed to be the future king of Israel. Prince Jonathan laid everything at the feet of David because Jonathan was kingdom-minded. Not his kingdom, but God's kingdom.

David never chose to be king; God chose David to be king. David was dedicated to the will of his father, which was to shepherd and protect his father's flock. When the devouring animals came to kill the little lambs, David protected the flock and killed the lion and the bear. When the sheep were restless, David pulled out his harp and began to play and sing under the anointing of God, and bring peace in the middle of the night. God saw these attributes in David and said, "This is a young man with the right heart to lead my people."

Peter, who had a reputation for being out of control at times, found himself with the 11 other disciples in a boat in the middle of the night on the Sea of Galilee. The Bible says in Matthew 14:24 that they were in a ship *"in the midst of the sea, tossed with waves; for the winds were contrary."* In the middle of that darkest hour, Jesus came walking on the water. The disciples seeing Him, filled with fear, thought that what they saw was just a ghost, but Jesus said, *"Be of good cheer, it is I; be not afraid"* (v.27). It was Peter who said, *"Lord, if it is You, command me to come to You on the water"* (v. 28). Now the big question: will he get out of the boat or stay in it? These disciples would not have thought less of him if he would have stayed in the boat. It was safer, it was acceptable, and it made sense. Most folks are most comfortable in the boat. There was something in Peter that gave him a strong confidence in the miraculous. Not just seeing it for others, not just watching what the Lord would do, he wanted to be a part of it. So, Peter steps out, and he is walking on the water! He is human, he probably moved slowly and he may have held on to the ship for as long as he could. At some point, you will let go of what is safe and acceptable, and reach for what is life- changing and supernatural.

This world is sick of religion. This world is so full of religion it is coming out of their ears. What they are not seeing but yet are hungry for is the demonstration and power of the almighty God. That power is inside of every believer, with signs of that power following the believers. In the name of Jesus Christ, they shall cast out devils, they shall speak with new tongues, they shall have power over the dangerous powers over nature, and they shall lay hands on the sick, and they shall recover (see Mark 16:17-18). *"These signs shall follow them that believe,"* and we are believers. We are not just church attendees and we are not just religionists; we are believers!

Peter walked in the realm of the miraculous with the Creator of all nature. Jesus placed into Peter's hand the keys to the kingdom of Heaven, based on the decision that Peter made. It is only two chapters later, beginning at Matthew 16:13, that Jesus asks His disciples, *"'Whom do men say that I am? So they said, 'Some say John the Baptist, some Elijah, and others Jeremiah or one of the prophets.' He said to them, 'But who do you say that I am?'"* Who answered this question? Peter! *"Simon Peter answered and said, 'You are the Christ, the Son of the living God.' Jesus answered and said to him, 'Blessed are you, Simon Bar-Jonah, for flesh and blood has not revealed this to you, but My Father who is in heaven. And I also say to you that you are Peter, and on this rock, I will build my church, and the gates of Hell shall not prevail against it. And I will give you the keys of the kingdom of heaven, and whatever you bind on earth will be bound in heaven, and whatever you loose on earth will be loosed in heaven.'"* This Scripture is a great faith-builder for all of us, but who received it first? Who was told personally by Jesus "I give you the keys to the kingdom of heaven?" Peter! I submit to you the keys were given because of the choice that Peter made.

God's choices are made based on the choices we make. I want to be used by God. There is nothing really left in this world except the power of God. *"By this you know the Spirit of God; every spirit that confesses that Jesus Christ is come in the flesh is of God, and every spirit that does not confess that Jesus Christ has come in the flesh is not of God. And this is the spirit of the Antichrist, which you have heard was coming, and is now already in the world. You are of God little children, and have overcome them, because greater is He that is in You, than He who is in the world"* (1 John 4:2-4). There is nothing greater in the world than what has been given to us as believers. There is not a religion, terrorist group, president, king or dictator that has power as great as what has already been given to us as believers. The devil and all of his angels, demons, principalities, and powers are absolutely no match for the power of God that has already been given to us as believers. You have been authorized to use the name of Jesus Christ! At the name of Jesus, devils tremble, hell shakes, and knees bow! You have hands for healing, voices for commanding, hearts to receive Divine revelation, a sanctified mind to comprehend God's will, and Holy Ghost power to declare the Word of the Lord!

We choose to pray. We choose to worship. We choose to live holy. We choose. This is not a feeling statement, this is a commitment statement. You know to do it, so do it! It is written to clap your hands. It is written to dance. It is written to pray. It is written to rejoice. It is written to praise Him with a loud voice. It is written to lift up holy hands. It is written, "Oh, magnify the Lord with me!" So, do it! You know to do it, so do it! You do not have to feel it, just do it. Why? Because God inhabits (dwells in) the praises of His people (Psalm 22:3)! If we build a big house of praise, He will come and dwell here in a great big way!

There is some misunderstanding about how and when to praise the Lord. I've had people say to me, "I do not do anything in church until I feel it." Where is that in the Bible? Please show me one place in the Bible where you only worship God when you "feel" it. If you wait until you feel it, you might not ever have a praise. Drop the self-centered attitude. As believers, we are continually in the presence of the Almighty King. And, *"where the Spirit of the Lord is, there is liberty"* (2 Corinthians 3:17).

In 2 Kings Chapter 3, we find three kings desiring a prophetic word from Elisha. But Elisha said, "I do not care who you are, I do not have a word for you today — I do not feel it." But does the story end there? No. Elisha said, *"But now bring me a minstrel. And it came to pass, when the minstrel played, that the hand of the Lord came upon him"* (v.15). When the musician played, the spirit of the prophet was stirred. Why do we open every service with music? Anointed music ushers in the presence of the Lord. For those who think that something is missing in your church service … start worshiping God. Sometimes nothing miraculous happens in the worship service because there are no true worshipers in the service. Worship opens the soul of man to the Spirit of God.

Moses was faithful. He trekked with those unbelieving Israelites for 40 years. Then God made a choice: "Moses, you cannot enter into the promised land." That must have been shattering news. After all, it was Moses who declared, "Let my people go." It was Moses who stretched out his rod and parted the Red Sea. It was Moses who prayed down manna, found water in a rock, lifted up the serpent of brass for their healing, and had decades of stress with ungrateful, critical followers. But he was prohibited from being the leader when the Israelites stepped into their Promised Land. Fast-forward to Mark chapter nine. Jesus took Peter, James and John to a high mountain and *"was transfigured before them"* (v.2). *"And there appeared unto them Elijah with Moses; and they were talking with Jesus"* (v.4). Moses may not have walked in the Promised Land during his life, but now we see Him standing in Promised Land, ministering to Jesus Christ. Whatever choice God makes for you, do it. In the end, you will receive everything you have been promised. Are you willing to give up everything to God? Everything you give to God will be given back to you and so much more. *"Peter said, 'See, we have left all and followed You.' So Jesus said to them, 'Assuredly, I say to you, there is no one who has left house or parents or brothers or wife or children, for the sake of the*

Kingdom of God, who shall not receive many times more in this present time, and in the age to come eternal life'" (Luke 18:28-30).

I choose to live for God. I choose to worship. I choose to pray. It is my own free will. It is my choice. People want to hear a Word from God, and I believe God is speaking now more than ever before. The Bible says in Revelation 2:7, 3:6, 3:13, and 3:22, *"He who has an ear, let him hear what the Spirit says to the churches."* Be willing to cancel out all the noise and the chaos of the world, and listen only to the voice of the Lord. Peter made every step safely while walking on the water until He paid attention to the storm. Keep your eyes on the Master. It is your choice.

THE FINAL HOUR

"Whose voice then shook the earth: but now He has promised, saying, 'Yet once more I shake not only the earth, but also heaven.' And this word, 'Yet once more', indicates the removal of those things that are being shaken, as of things that are made, that the things which cannot be shaken may remain. Therefore, since we are receiving a kingdom which cannot be shaken, let us have grace, by which we may serve God acceptably with reverence and godly fear. For our God is a consuming fire" (Hebrews 12:26-29). We are at this time right now. I see the biggest shaking in the spirit world of any time I have ever seen in nearly 30 years of being a Christian. I declare to you that we, the people of God, sealed by the Holy Ghost until the day of redemption, are not going to be shaken loose. It is easy to talk about a wicked world; it is easy to make negative comments about the church across town whose worship service looks differently than yours. Actually, this is another of Satan's blinding techniques. I submit to you that those who do know their God clearly see our time and opportunity, and are rising up in strength and doing exploits. I hear the sound of an abundance of rain, I hear the sound of a rushing mighty wind, I hear the crackle of cloven tongues of fire; I hear the cry that says we have come to the Kingdom of God for such a time as this. You have been called — chosen by God — and this is our hour!

Those who are fighting the Spirit of God are being revealed for their false works. Sincere believers are done with flesh, sincere believers are done with programs, and sincere believers are done with dead religion. Sincere believers still love the altar. Sincere believers still love true worship. Sincere believers still love preaching that is accompanied by the power and demonstration of the Spirit. God is withholding nothing! If you are in the ministry for any reason other than souls, you will not be successful in the Kingdom, and you will be shaken loose.

CHAPTER 9

A CHANGED MIND

"Now after six days Jesus took Peter, James, and John his brother, led them up on a high mountain by themselves; and He was transfigured before them. His face shone like the sun, and His clothes became as white as the light. And behold, Moses and Elijah appeared to them, talking with Him. Then Peter answered and said to Jesus, 'Lord, it is good for us to be here; if You wish, let us make here three tabernacles: one for You, one for Moses, and one for Elijah.' While he was still speaking, behold, a bright cloud overshadowed them; and suddenly a voice came out of the cloud, saying, 'This is My beloved Son, in whom I am well pleased. Hear Him'" (Matthew 17:1-5)!

Each one of the four gospels presents Jesus in a certain perspective, and in Matthew's writings, he shows Christ as the King of the Jews. Matthew uses an active method of writing — a teaching narrative that presents Jesus in an environment that gives us the revelation of Christ, showing us how people reacted to Him in those encounters. It shows us who we are and who He is in a dynamic way. In other words, in His encounters with people, Jesus intends for us to be challenged. But Christ never challenged anyone to lose; it was and always is for the purpose to gain. Of course, some people get offended, but His purpose is to shake the foundation of our normalcy — what we regard as our "comfort zone."

After Jesus and these select three came down from the mountain, *"a certain man came to Jesus and said, 'Lord have mercy on my son, for he is an epileptic* (King James Version uses the word lunatic) *and suffers severely; for he often falls in to the fire and often into the water. So I brought him to Your disciples, but they could not cure Him.' Then Jesus answered and said, 'O faithless and perverse generation, how long shall I be with you? How long shall I bear with you? Bring him here to Me.' And Jesus rebuked the demon, and it came out of him, and the child was cured from that very hour. Then the disciples came to Jesus privately and said, 'Why could we not cast it out?' So Jesus said to them, 'Because of your unbelief....'"* (vs. 14-20). The people who were with Jesus intensely for three years still struggled to move to the level that Jesus desired for them to experience.

The disciples could not heal the man's son, and yet they were with Jesus all the time. Here is a question: How long does it take and how much do I have to receive from God to get to the point that I consistently and faithfully stand on the Word of God in every situation in my life and believe Him like I should? This is faith because it takes faith to move from where I am across the bridge to where He is. When Jesus asked the man in John 5:6, *"Will you be made whole?",* He was specifically asking Him, "Do you have the capacity to receive what I have to give you — do you accept what I am about to put in your hand?" Jesus does not give anything that is not received. Many times church folk misrepresent Jesus because we spend more time dealing with our traditions than in introducing the power of Christ. In the 21st century, we have spent more time dealing with health, wealth and prosperity, and little time dealing with a true relationship with Jesus Christ.

I submit to you that in our self-professed efforts of not being religious, we have simply switched from one form of religion to another. If our message is not about the power of God transforming lives, then it is just religion. In the past 50 years, many in the Pentecostal Holiness movement have switched from the thinking of God's people who live in true holiness will be poor and ridiculed and have small churches and dress conservatively. Now, some have traded the style of plain clothing and no jewelry to excessive clothing and jewelry debts (and minimum payments on excessive credit card balances). We speak in tongues, so we think we must have an inside track with God. We tend to think that if someone really walks in faith, then everything will be grand every day. All of that is just religion — we have just painted it a different color in the 21st century. Christ was, is, and always will be looking for people to save, heal, deliver, set free, and forever change by the power of His blood.

Back to our story — you will see that it was the dad that came to Jesus. Quick question: Why didn't the disciples come and get Jesus when they could not get the job done? Quick answer: Too many people enjoy the status of being around Jesus and the status of being important (which is exactly what the disciples were hooked on) while hurting people keep on hurting. If you think about it, the disciples never really looked good in the Scriptures. They could not heal this man's son; they tried to keep the little children away from Jesus; they tried to shut up the Syrophoenician woman that kept pleading for help, just to name a few.

Three words of advice for readers who may be new Christians:
1. Beware of religious people that do not have a Kingdom mentality.
2. You never, ever get to the place where you do not need Jesus.
3. Do not ever forget the power of Christ in your life.

A seldom told story begins in Matthew 15:32 where Jesus fed 4000 men plus the women and children with seven loaves of bread and a few fish. But, only one chapter later, Jesus says, *"'...Take heed and beware of the leaven of the Pharisees and the Sadducees.' And they reasoned among themselves, saying, 'It is because we have taken no bread.' But Jesus, being aware of it, said to them, 'O you of little faith, why do you reason among yourselves because you have brought not bread? Do you not yet understand, or remember the five loaves of the five thousand ... nor the seven loaves of the four thousand ... How is it you do not understand that I do not speak concerning bread'"* (Matthew 16:6-11)? How easily the power of Christ is forgotten when a new crisis shows up!

How long do we walk with God until we speak to every mountain, not just those little mountains that we have already dealt with? How long do we walk with God, yet struggle with 20-year-old issues? How long do we still deal with the same habits that the devil has convinced us we cannot get rid of? How long do we still let the same hurts pull us down over and over again?

Even after Jesus had risen from the dead, that same mindset shows up again. The disciples asked Jesus, *"Lord, will you now restore again the kingdom of Israel"* (Acts 1:6)? I think if I were Jesus, I would have fired every one of them on the spot! But Jesus says, "No, the Father has all of that taken care of. You go to the Upper Room, stay there until the power of the Holy Ghost comes upon you, and go preach." Focus on the Kingdom of God, not on the kingdoms of this world! This world desperately needs anointed believers to preach the Word, save the lost, heal the sick, cast out devils, and raise the dead!

DECISION MAKERS

The experiences you have had were not for nothing. Experiences have meaning. Experiences leave deposits. The question is: What do you do with your life deposits? Satan would love to destroy you by depositing destruction into your spirit. If we allow the enemy to deposit doubt and anger and envy and strife and jealousy and lust into our lives, there comes a change in the mindset. Our mindset is no longer about "What does God want?" it changes to "What do I want?"

"Follow peace with all men, and holiness, without which no one shall see the Lord. Looking carefully lest anyone shall fall short of the grace of God; lest any root of bitterness springing up cause trouble, and by this many become defiled, lest there be any fornicator or profane person like Esau, who for one morsel of food sold his birthright. For you know that afterward, when he wanted to inherit the blessing, he was rejected, for he found no place for repentance, though he sought it diligently with tears" (Hebrews 12:14-17).

Though we always say, "the God of Abraham, Isaac, and Jacob," in reality, the correct lineage would be "the God of Abraham, Isaac, and

Esau." Esau was Isaac's first-born and thus he was the rightful heir. He was the one that should have received all the spiritual blessings as the first-born of Isaac and as the grandson of Abraham, along with the conveying of property and all of the rights and goods and opportunities and influence. Esau lost it all because he was hungry. He came back from a hunting trip, and his brother Jacob had a bowl of soup. Because Esau was hungry, Jacob made a deal — a bowl of soup for his birthright. We preach it as being tricked; I think it is more accurate to say that Esau was dumb. It would be like me offering to trade you my new bicycle for your new truck. If you agree to that even trade, I did not trick you; you are just dumb! What was dumb? Esau made a permanent decision based on a temporary situation. We cannot blame all of our problems on "the tricks of the enemy." A lot of our problems are because we do dumb stuff. I have done some of the dumbest stuff! I have asked myself so many times, "How in the world could you have done something so dumb?" We can make decisions about a 30-minute situation that ends up having a 30-year impact.

Read verse 17 again: *"... Afterward, when he wanted to inherit the blessing, he was rejected, for he found no place for repentance, though he sought it diligently with tears."* He lost his future, not because of a mistake, but because of what he had set in motion over his life. All of us have done dumb things. The real question is, do we stay there? I submit to you that Esau must have had a pattern of making dumb decisions; otherwise, Jacob would not have had the thought to offer him so little for so much.

Esau sought repentance but did not find it. That sounds illogical until we consider it further. The truest definition of repentance, taken from the original Greek "metanoia," is the "passing over of the mind." Quite simply, repentance is changing your mind about something or someone. Esau found no place for repentance though he had many tears. So, an emotional response does not equate to change. Crying or feeling bad about a situation or mistake or life crisis is not repentance until there is a changed mindset. Perhaps you have heard this before: "There is nothing as powerful as a changed mind." The enemy is no longer in control when you change your mind.

"This I say, therefore, and testify in the Lord, that you should no longer walk as the rest of the Gentiles walk, in the futility of their mind, having their understanding darkened, being alienated from the life of God, because of the ignorance that is in them, because of the blindness of their heart; who, being past feeling, have given themselves over to lewdness, to work all uncleanness with greediness. But you have not so learned Christ, if indeed you have heard Him and have been taught by Him, as the truth is in Jesus: that you put off, concerning your former conduct, the old man which grows corrupt according to the deceitful lusts, **and be renewed in the spirit of your mind,** *and that you put on the new man which was created according to God, in true righteousness and holiness"* (Ephesians 4:17-24 emphasis added).

The biggest fight that you will ever have is in your mind. Though there are a lot of things you will deal with, the hardest battles in life are in the mind. *"For though we walk in the flesh, we do not war according to the flesh. For the weapons of our warfare are not carnal, but mighty in God for pulling down strongholds, casting down arguments and every high thing that exalts itself against the knowledge of God, bringing every thought into captivity to the obedience of Christ, and being ready to punish all disobedience when your obedience is fulfilled"* (2 Corinthians 10:3-6). Your spirit man is ready! Your spirit man is full of the Holy Ghost, and the Bible says that the spirit inside of you is prepared to punish all disobedience, as you walk in obedience to the Word of God. What does that mean? When the mind heads off in the wrong direction, the Spirit of God inside of you rises up in power and declares, "No!"

Those things in our mind that argue against God's Word or that tries to exalt itself against God's Word are pulled down. They are brought into captivity to become obedient. Furthermore, you will also deal with things that are not sin but yet are not in alignment with God's will. In your mind, you will deal with depression, you will deal with fear, you will deal with negative thoughts that are not necessarily sin, but yet they are a product of sin that came from the fall of Adam. There are a lot of people that are held captive to things in their mind, while Christ is saying, "I have made you free!"

In the well-known parable of The Prodigal Son in Luke chapter 15, we find a young man in a hog pen, broke, deranged, deprived, and distraught. But the Bible says in verse 17 that *"he came to himself."* No one came to his rescue, he did not receive a letter with money in the mail, and he did not retain the services of a personal life coach. Rather, "he came to himself." There was a moment of clarity that came in his mind, and he said, "Hey, I do not have to live this way." With clarity of mind came a change — he got up and got out. There was only one key to his liberty — it was a realization of the truth that occurred in his mind. How did he get there to begin with? Because in his mind, he developed a fantasy of how great life would be in the "far country." That is where all the fun is. That is where all the really cool guys and gals are. That is where there is a party every night. Everyone will like me there. I won't have any rules. No one will tell me what to do. I can do whatever I want to whenever I feel like it. And, for the most part, that was all true! As an independent adult, you can do what you want. There is always a party somewhere if you look for it. There will always be a cute girl or guy ready to get it on. For the Prodigal Son, in all of that freedom came bondage, a bondage that was in his mind. All he did was take the old man to a new place. When the old man shows up in a new place he will have the same old problems there as he did where he came from.

People try all kinds of tactics to deal with their problem instead of The One solution that will change everything. If a man has a problem with lust, getting married will not solve that problem. If you have a problem with lust before you are married, you will have a problem with lust after you are married. If you have a drug problem in Kentucky, you will have a drug problem if you move to Texas. If you have money problems when you are making $25,000 a year, you will have money problems when you make $250,000 a year.

The difference between David and Esau is the same difference that we see between Peter and Judas. Every one of these men failed and every one of these men repented, but every one of these men did not change. Esau was sorry and he cried bitterly but he never changed. Judas was seized with remorse and returned the 30 pieces of silver he had been given in his betrayal of Jesus. He was sorry but he did not change. How do I know that? He threw the money at the elders and went and hanged himself (Matthew 27:3-5). What had he seen from Christ continually for the past three years? Grace, forgiveness, and mercy. But he allowed Satan to establish a stronghold in his mind. Spiritually, he became blind. Believing in his mind that he could not (or should not) be forgiven was a stronghold that caused his death. Not one suicide has ever been an accident. It is a physical action that is the product of an internal action performed in the mind.

David changed his mind. He said, "I will not be an adulterer and a murderer." And, the Bible says that David was a man after God's own heart. Peter changed his mind. And, Peter was the first bishop of the New Testament Church, who preached the revelation of the new dispensation of the church age so powerfully that 3000 people were converted and baptized. One of the main tenants of our Pentecostal faith comes out of this man's message in Acts chapter 2 after he was truly transformed and Spirit-filled.

An integral key to the believer's spiritual success is the awareness and capacity to change our minds. We do not fear the work of Satan against us. If you are covered by the blood of Jesus Christ and sealed until the Day of Redemption by the Spirit of God, then I am assured beyond any doubt that spiritual victory and a blessed life is a covenant promise guaranteed by Jehovah God.

With our spiritual eyes wide open, we have the blessed assurance of the great Romans 8:35 promise that *"nothing shall separate us from the love of God!"* The enemy of our soul has been determined to prevent every living person from a relationship with God. He has failed millions of times throughout the centuries, and I trust that his plans against you and I fail completely. My purpose in this book is to both remind and instruct us that our spiritual focus does not have to be consumed with devils and demons and the like. My biggest enemy can be the guy I look at in the mirror every morning.

If I am happy in my faith, outward circumstances can trouble my mind but never touch my spirit.

If I live a life of communication with God, I will see every situation against the backdrop of His Word.

If I give thanks in everything, the spirit of dissatisfaction will not distract me.

If I am committed to holiness and sanctification, sin will not extinguish the fire of the Holy Ghost in my life.

If I love the Word, then the lure of worldliness will never overpower my walk with Christ.

If I embrace unity, then differences will not bring separation.

If grace is my teacher, I will live a life of transformation.

If my spiritual eyes are wide open, no enemy has any chance of being successful.

PROLOGUE

"Paul, I have something to tell you." Tears are flowing freely down the face of my dear young brother in the faith. "Timothy, my son. Why are you so troubled? Tell me, now!"

"Demas." The name is choked out in a near whisper.

"What of Demas? Is he ill? Is he …," I refuse to say out loud the next thought that came to my mind.

"No, sir. He is not sick, nor is he dead." He knew what I was afraid to say. "Demas has left us."

"Left us? Where did he go? I have not seen him for a few weeks. I thought perhaps he had found another village to preach. You know how focused he becomes when he finds open ears and hungry hearts." I almost chuckle at the zeal I have seen in Demas in our past travels, but Timothy's face gives me a reason to refrain. I ask again, "Where is Demas?"

"He has gone back to Thessalonica."

"Thessalonica? What is he doing there? He told me many times that he would never return to his home place! The Lord must have a great work for him there!"

"Paul, Demas has not gone back to Thessalonica to witness for the Lord. Demas has gone back because he no longer is witnessing for the Lord. I have been concerned for some time now. I tried to talk to him, but he kept putting me off or avoiding me altogether. I did not know he was leaving! Luke received word from the brethren there ...." The rest of what he tried to say was lost in the silence of disappointment.

I turn away from the window. The responsibility to properly respond to my young protégé outweighs my desire to grieve. "Spirit of God, show me what to do...."

"Timothy, listen carefully! Please go fetch my books and papers. I need to study and write. Bring my coat, as well. The nights are getting cool in this place. Hurry along, now. We will talk more about Demas when you return."

Timothy gives me a curious look as he wipes his face, but quickly disappears into the crowded morning streets. I know he will be gone for a couple of hours. Just enough time to leave him my most personal letter. This is the letter that the Lord will use to sustain and keep him and perhaps many others after I am gone.

I pull out the few remaining strips of paper I have left in this old prison cell, sharpen my quill and adjust the small candle. As I breathe a prayer for clarity and encouragement, the words begin to flow....

Timothy,

I solemnly urge you in the presence of God and Christ Jesus, who will someday judge the living and the dead when he comes to set up his Kingdom, to preach the word of God! Always be prepared, whether the time is favorable or not. Patiently correct, rebuke, and encourage your people with good teaching. For a time is coming when people will no longer listen to sound and wholesome teaching. They will follow their own desires and will look for teachers who will tell them whatever their itching ears want to hear. They will reject the truth and chase after myths. But you should keep a clear mind in every situation. Do not be afraid of suffering for the Lord. Work at telling others the Good News and fully carry out the ministry God has given you.

As for me, my life has already been poured out as an offering to God. The time of my death is near. I have fought the good fight, I have finished the race, and I have remained faithful. And now the prize awaits me — the crown of righteousness, which the Lord, the righteous Judge, will give me on the day of His return. The prize is not just for me but for all who eagerly look forward to his appearing.

I know you are disappointed, as I am, about Demas. We will pray the Lord speak boldly to his heart, for Demas loves the things of this life. Others have disappointed me along the way, especially Alexander the coppersmith. He did me much harm, but the Lord will judge him for what he has done. Be careful of him, for he fought against everything we said.

I appreciate your faithful companionship. The first time I was brought before the judge, no one came with me and everyone abandoned me. May it not be counted against them. But the Lord stood with me and gave me strength so that I might preach the Good News in its entirety for all the Gentiles to hear. He rescued me from certain death, and the Lord will deliver me from every evil attack and will me safely into His heavenly Kingdom. All glory to God forever and ever! Amen.

I love you and the many dear friends who have stood faithfully with me. Please express my deepest gratitude to all who have shared with me in the fellowship of the gospel.

May the Lord be with your spirit with all grace. [9]

Until we see Him face to face,

Paul

REFERENCES

1. Psalm 138, KJV

2. "Can't Nobody Hide from God" is a traditional gospel blues song recorded in 1930 by Blind Willie Johnson and Willie B. Harris. It was released as a single on Columbia Records.

3. Lyrics by Bernie Brillstein, Frank Peppiatt, and John Aylesworth. Recorded by Buck Owens and Roy Clark.

4. "Again I Say Rejoice" Israel Houghton, Aaron Lindsey © 2004 Integrity's Praise! Music/Sound Of The New Breed Publishing

5. History/Doctrine of PCG: Our Story. Aaron Wilson. Messenger Publishing House

6. Greg Stier, "Over 300,000 Churches in America: Do We Really Need More Church Plants?" *The Christian Post.* February 16, 2016

7. Barna Group, "The State of the Church 2016."

8. "Grace, the Forbidden Gospel" Andre van der Merwe. www.ntslibrary.com 2011

9. Includes sections of 2 Timothy 4, NLT

www.ingramcontent.com/pod-product-compliance
Lightning Source LLC
Chambersburg PA
CBHW021442080526
44588CB00009B/641